Our Struggles Have Purpose

50+ Life Lessons From My Walk with Cancer

By

Shawn Elizabeth George

Foreword by

Stephen George

Live from the Inside Out, LLC
All rights reserved.
ISBN: 0998302937
ISBN-13: 978-0998302935

Cover and author picture by Peter J Marzano of www.secretlakephotography.com

Editing done by Rita M. Reali of www.persnicketyproofreader.wordpress.com

OTHER BOOKS BY SHAWN ELIZABETH GEORGE

MY JOURNEY TO LIVE FROM THE INSIDE OUT

A PLACE FOR SAM (A CHILDREN'S BOOK)

DEDICATION

This book is dedicated to the circles of love that wrapped me, and our family, in love and prayer throughout our walk with cancer. Thank you from the bottom of my heart for who you are and for showing up for our family in our time of need.

And to my Inner Circles…

Stephen
You are the kids' and my rock covered in laughter.
You bring calm and joy even into life's toughest storms.

Kate, Gavin and Matthew
You are my heart, my loves, my joys.
Your loving, brave and courageous hearts inspire me every day.

Mom and Dad
There are no words that can express the gratitude in my heart for all you mean to me and for all you have done for us.

Petey, Tricia, Kathy, Barbara, Paula Sue and your families
Thank you for always being there.
Your love and support are felt every day, in every way.

Claire and Steve
I know why Stephen always shows up for our family.
You showed him the way.

My Sacred Seven
Thank you for always hearing my heart and for praying for our family, even when I didn't know how to.

FOREWORD

I don't think it was until the day after Shawn's initial diagnosis that I talked to my parents about the news. I called them on my way home from work and my mom answered the phone. I'm pretty sure that she knew right away that something wasn't right. At first I couldn't even respond when she asked how Shawn's appointment had gone. Eventually I was able to tell her that it wasn't good news. I actually couldn't say the word "cancer." That was a really tough word to say. More than one year later, "cancer" is a word we've grown accustomed to, and it's a lot easier to say it these days. Cancer has become part of our family's life.

We didn't choose to go on this walk with cancer, but I think that this walk was chosen for us. If you know Shawn, you know that she *loves* to take long walks, sometimes very l-o-n-g ones. Even though I haven't always been a willing participant to go on these walks, we've been on many together. This walk that we have been on, our walk with cancer, has been very different than the others. As we make our way down this path, each day we find ourselves moving along different twists and turns. As we continue on, it becomes more and more clear that this walk doesn't ever really end.

It wasn't until recently that I began to really mentally process the events of the past year. Sounds odd, but it is true. From the initial diagnosis on that cold day in January through the ringing of the bell signaling the end of Shawn's radiation treatments on a warm day in June, it felt like we were on a mission. I felt like there was no time for reflection and processing in the midst of the battle. Writing this foreword has turned out to be an essential part of my processing all we have been through.

I knew it in my heart from the beginning that Shawn was going to be fine, I was confident of that. No matter what happened, I knew that Shawn was meant to make good of this situation. This was her focus from the start. This book is part of how she is going to make good of having cancer.

Only the day before her diagnosis we returned from a long weekend together in Nashville. We had a great time relaxing together, bar-hopping and listening to great music along the way. We walked a lot. One day we walked ten miles. (I told you she likes long walks.) It didn't take long after the trip to Nashville for things to change quickly.

The day after we returned, there we were in Dr. Tessema's office, listening half-intently and half-dazed, as he explained that something wasn't quite right and he was concerned. He didn't like what he saw. The sinus issues that Shawn had experienced for months weren't going to be resolved by a nasal spray – not even close. It became clear that we were about to embark upon a journey, potentially a long one, from the way he was talking. He explained to us that we were only on step one of many steps. His advice was to stay on the step that we were on. I would repeat this advice to myself, and we would repeat it to each other, numerous times over the year to come.

On the way to pick up our three kids after the appointment we stopped at church. We sat in a pew on the side of the church, not where we usually sat on Sundays (usually we are in the back with the other late arrivals). I remember pointing out to Shawn that we had unintentionally positioned ourselves between two stained glass windows. One had a depiction of St. Francis, the other was of St. Jude. It felt good to have ended up here. St. Francis was the name of the hospital in Hartford where Shawn had given birth to our three incredible children and St. Jude is a name synonymous with amazing cancer care. It seemed like a good seat to be in that day...maybe we had someone keeping an eye on us along this walk that lay ahead.

Shawn and I made a decision early on that we would be as honest and forthcoming as we could be with our kids. Even though they were young and this would be tough for them, we wanted them to be able to understand what was happening to their mom.

Unfortunately we didn't get off to a great start being honest with them.

Over the years we had developed a routine after each school concert. After the choir had sung its songs, and after the strings and the band had played their final tunes, we'd head out to a local ice cream shop to celebrate. Shawn had a number of tests to go through over the days following our unsettling meeting with Dr. Tessema. One of those tests was an MRI which was scheduled after our son's winter concert. Immediately following the concert, it didn't feel quite right when we told the kids we were going out for a date night. (It also didn't make much sense given that we'd just returned from a weekend in Nashville.) We both wondered what they must be thinking. There was no ice cream celebration that night. That night the kids headed home with one of Shawn's sisters while Shawn and I headed off for our "night on the town." The ice cream celebration with our kids was replaced by a late night MRI 30 minutes away at the only location where we could get an appointment that day.

It was from that point on that we decided we'd be honest with the kids, and though we wouldn't tell them everything, everything we told them was going to be the truth. This felt like the right plan, for us anyway. The five of us were going to be on this walk together - for better, or for worse.

We had many others along with us on this walk. The offers of help from others; family, friends, strangers even, were immediate, amazing, and overwhelming at times. Initially, because I didn't know any better, I didn't want any help. I was pretty sure that we could manage this on our own. We'd been through tough times in our time together - we could handle this. The thing is that we really didn't know what was to come.

Knowing that people would be inundating us with food (because that is what people do apparently) over the coming months, my parents offered to buy us a second refrigerator to help store it all. It was a good idea, but I was sure we didn't need help. After a few more offers to buy that refrigerator I went out one morning and bought one myself. We had this covered on our own, I was still pretty sure of that.

It took a while to realize that it was okay to accept help. We didn't have to do this on our own. Shawn's sisters setup a meal train on a website. Looking back, I'm not sure what we would have done without it. I may never again eat another piece of lasagna, but that's a small price to pay for the overwhelming generosity of others that showed up on our doorstep seemingly every evening.

The day before Shawn's surgery at Massachusetts Eye and Ear Infirmary in Boston we said a long, tearful goodbye to the kids and drove up to Boston to ride out an impending mid-March blizzard. I think they wondered what mom would be like when she returned - I guess we all did a little. We had gone to see several doctors to get opinions on how best to attack this cancer. We visited some of the best doctors in the world in Boston and New York. Boston had felt like the right place from the very beginning and we had a lot of peace with our decision.

The afternoon before the surgery, in the blowing snow, Shawn and I walked from our hotel that overlooked Boston Harbor in Charlestown over to Mass Eye and Ear. Shawn would end up walking this same path dozens of time during her treatments, sometimes with me, and sometimes with another friend or family member who had come to keep her company for the week. She never walked alone. This same path, along the harbor's edge, under the Zakim Bridge, through North Point Park and its playground, past the Boston Science Center and down Storrow Drive would become a familiar one. Shawn would use this same hotel as home base for her stay while she completed her seven weeks of radiation and chemotherapy treatments. We developed a fondness for Boston, the city and its people, that I'm sure will last a lifetime.

Sitting in the hotel room on the night before the surgery, eating popcorn and staring blankly at the television, we couldn't help but recall how our emotions were remarkably familiar to us. They were similar to those we'd felt in the days leading up to my departure years ago for Navy boot camp or how we felt on those long nights before long submarine deployments. The feeling was intense, filled with a sense of great unknown and, even though the journey had not yet begun, a longing for a return to normalcy. Throughout those ten long weeks of boot camp, and on each of my submarine deployments, Shawn had been by my side without fail. Her support was constant and unwavering. I was determined to return the favor. Of course, I would be by her side on her walk, and on this mission that united us and our family, immediate and extended alike, on what was a common goal. There could be no other way.

On the morning of her surgery, Shawn's parents and I sat with her as the surgical team prepared. She asked me to make note of the names of those that were part of the team. Not just the names of the doctors, she asked, but of everyone, from the names of each nurse to the name of the man who rolled her bed into the operating room. We needed the names so we would be prepared to come back and thank them all later. They all had a part to play in her journey. Shawn was determined to make sure that they all understood that their role, however small, was important to her. This is part of how Shawn was going to make good of all this.

Shawn is an intense competitor, a fighter. If you've ever played her in one-on-one basketball, or even in a friendly game of cards, you know this. She doesn't go down without a fight. This has never been more evident than it was in the days and weeks after the surgery. It was not easy. For weeks she "ate" her liquid meals from a small 5 mL syringe, re-learning how to swallow while the wounds were still healing, and as she got adjusted to her new artificial palate. Having Shawn back at home was a chance to regroup and get ready for the next step while the healing continued.

Seven weeks of radiation and chemotherapy began in Boston in early May. Springtime in Boston had a certain allure to it, we were hopeful and looking forward to getting started. The winter dragged on though, and the warmer spring days were few and far between as winter held on as long as it could. Shawn spent the weekdays in Boston and returned home for weekends with the kids and me. This time at home with the kids was critical. They had been amazing through all of this, and a couple days with mom helped recharge their spirits for the upcoming week.

In the days since Shawn's surgery and treatment, I've explained our walk through those months beginning with her surgery on March 15 and ending with the ringing of the bell signaling the end of her treatment on June 22 as being similar to a long submarine deployment. Early in the journey it is not uncommon to be overwhelmed by what lies ahead. As time goes on, the routine becomes the routine. You put your head down and push through, not thinking beyond today, taking just one day at a time. As you get close to the end, the excitement of the return home begins to build and you intently start counting the remaining days.

The kids, Shawn's parents, and I were there by her side on June 22 when she rang the bell at Massachusetts General Hospital in the lobby of the Francis H. Burr Proton Therapy Center, signaling the end of her treatment. We all walked back down Storrow Drive, past the Boston Science Center, through North Point Park where the kids played on the playground, under the Zakim Bridge, along the harbor's edge back to the hotel. We were on to the next step.

School was out, and summertime was upon us immediately. Vacations had been planned, life had to go on. We didn't plan well for the healing that still needed to occur. Treatment was over, but there was still healing to be done. As we have learned, the radiation, the chemo, and the entire walk to this point takes an immeasurable toll. Healing does not end with the ringing of the bell. In fact, it may turn out to be the longest step in this journey.

In late August, we rented a vacation home for a week in the area of Acadia National Park in Maine. The location allowed for solitude and relaxation, mixed with outdoor adventure and much needed time together as a family. We walked and hiked Acadia's various trails nearly every day. Shawn went to bed early most nights and woke up later than usual; healing was still happening. We rented bikes and rode them through the park on the day of the late summer solar eclipse. We chose the easier bike trails but there were still many hills. On the longer hills Shawn would tend to fall behind. She was still working on regaining her strength and endurance. Just like she never gave up during her walk with cancer to this point, Shawn never gave up on those hills. The rest of us would tend to get a little ahead but we'd always circle back to wait for her on the side of the trail or ride by her side as she reached the top of the hill.

In many ways our lives have returned to normal. Earlier tonight we attended a spring concert at school for our son. Tomorrow night we will attend another one for our daughter. The ice cream celebration will wait until tomorrow because two nights of ice cream in a row is a bit much, at least that is what we had decided earlier tonight. I guess that I wasn't all that surprised to see Shawn passing out ice cream to the kids when we got home. These days she tends to not pass up an opportunity to celebrate. Her perspective on life has shifted a bit in the days since we began this walk in January of last year. You never know when the next chance to celebrate will be.

Shawn is what some people have described as an "old soul". She has wisdom, and a perspective on life, that sometimes seems like it is that of someone much older than she is. As someone who has been by Shawn's side as much as possible for over twenty years, I have benefitted from her wisdom and from her perspective on life that she shares intently with me and the kids every day. My wish for you as you begin reading this book is that you take away one thing that impacts your life, or someone else's life, in a positive manner. If every single person who reads this book takes away just one thing, then imagine how far that would go toward making good out of our walk with cancer. That is all Shawn has wished and prayed for since she was diagnosed; that something good would come from this.

For those of you that have been with us on this walk the entire way, or even for just a few steps along the way; thank you. We are forever grateful.

To our kids who have been by our side on this walk since the beginning; thank you. You have been amazing inspirations from the start. We love you guys more than you will ever know.

To Shawn who is still bravely walking the walk each day with grace, hope, and love; thank you. We will forever be by your side on this walk, no matter how long that is.

On to the next step...

\- Stephen

LIFE LESSONS

LIFE LESSON

1

EMBRACE THE TRUTH RATHER THAN THE STORIES WE CREATE

For eight months I had been experiencing a lot of congestion. I'd started snoring at night, which was driving Stephen crazy. I went to the doctor multiple times, yet what they suggested did not provide me with any relief. Things came to a head when I had four nights when I could not breathe through my nose. Literally no air would flow in, and no air would flow out. If I closed my mouth while sleeping, it felt like I was suffocating. It was awful.

For a while, my gut had said to find a new doctor. After those four rough nights and having had no relief, I finally found a new practice to go to. In my first appointment with this new practice, I was told this had been going on for too long and they thought it was best for me to go to an ENT – an ear, nose and throat specialist.

When the morning of my appointment with the ENT arrived I was tempted to cancel. Stephen and I had just been away and my nose felt a little less congested than it had been. Yet something in me said to go. So I listened to that inner voice and went.

When I walked into the office for my appointment, I expected to be walking out with nasal spray or some type of medicine.

My ENT, Dr. Tessema, examined me and, in his calm manner, said there was something he wanted me to see. On the computer screen he showed me a video of his examination. As he explained it, he should have been able to see the back of my nose but something was blocking him from going further. A growth, he called it. Then he showed me a picture of the back of my palate, where there was a lump.

I think my brain was still processing seeing the growth in my nose. Although my eyes saw the lump on the back of my palate he was pointing out, I am not sure I fully registered what I was seeing.

Calmly he shared that he wanted me to go to the building next door to get a CT scan, and asked that my husband accompany me back to another appointment later that same day, to discuss the findings from the scan.

What? A CT scan… today? Stephen needs to come back with me? This doesn't sound good. What's going on?

I called Stephen at work and explained the situation. He said he'd be there. I went to the next building for the CT scan. While I sat there waiting, my mind was in a loop, playing in slow motion the pictures Dr. Tessema had just shared with me.

What was happening?

The loop paused when the woman called my name.

On the way out of my CT scan, one of the women who had performed the scan said to me, "No matter what, remember you will be okay." She proceeded to share with me part of her story, which included being a breast-cancer survivor.

At that moment, I didn't realize why she shared that information, but now I know. She had seen something on my scan and knew I had a journey ahead of me.

When Stephen arrived, I gave him a huge hug. His presence brought a calm to the ping-ponging thoughts in my head.

Together we met with Dr. Tessema, who reviewed the findings of the scan with us. I had a tumor in my palate and nasal cavity (hence the snoring and trouble breathing through my nose, especially when I was congested). On the monitor, he showed us the tumor had already eroded bone – which meant it had been there for some time.

As I sat there, my thoughts swirling, uncertain of what it all meant, Dr. Tessema explained there were five steps I needed to go through, and right now we were on step one. I needed an MRI and biopsy to determine what exactly this tumor was.

Step 1. MRI and Biopsy.

Got it.

I 'got it' for a sliver of a second and then the whirlwind of thoughts bombarded me again.

What is this? What does this mean? Is this cancer? What is going on? I had a stuffy nose. Now I need an MRI? And a biopsy? What is happening?

During those first 48 hours, I existed in a numb state. It was as though the walls around me tightened in on me and fear took grip of my heart not letting me escape, even for a moment. My every thought centered around dying and the fact there was so much I had taken for granted – and so much I would not be able to do with my family in the future:

I always pictured growing old with Stephen, holding each other's wrinkled hands as we sat in our blue rocking chairs on the sand… someday.

I always expected to be there to watch our children grow up – and now I'd miss all the major milestones in their lives: graduations, weddings, watching their kids grow up, and more.

Yes, I saw my life pass by in the blink of an eye and, sadly, saw what our family of five would look like as a family of four. This was so *not* what I had planned. At one point I turned to Stephen in tears, saying I felt I was going to implode.

I love this life I have been given and the people I get to share it. I'm not ready to go, God. I want to be here. I want all those dreams to become my realities.

What is going on? Do I have cancer? Am I going to die?

The unknown. The uncertainty. The lack of control. It was all too much for me to absorb all at once.

Over that weekend as I waited for the scheduled biopsy – and over the next week, while I awaited the results – I realized I was creating a story for myself in my head that wasn't true. I was here, now. That was the truth. And it wasn't productive to spend my time with my eyes focused on the possibility that I had cancer and I was going to die.

I needed to…

Pause. Breathe. Pray.

And focus my eyes on God to help me get back on solid ground because I was in quicksand and getting swallowed up swiftly.

When I chose to lift my eyes from the problem and focus my eyes on God, it was like He invited me into the eye of the storm. I had been swept away in the whirlwind of the chaos, yet He wanted me to be still. He wanted to calm the storm in my mind and focus me back on truth.

Yes, I have a tumor – but that isn't who I am. The truth is, I am a wife, mother, daughter, sister, cousin, aunt and friend. I need to be who I am – and not allow this bone-eroding tumor to define me.

Yes, there is so much I don't know. Yet, if I dwell there, which is a natural place to go, I know it will lead me to a dark and heavy place. I've been there before in life, and I didn't want to head back there.

Yes, this news turned me upside-down. I was so full of fear, at times my body would literally shake uncontrollably, because I was so unnerved by what was happening. But was staying in that place going to help me – let alone my husband or my children – through this time?

Yes, cancer may have invaded my body, but it doesn't need to touch my Spirit.

The reality was those stories I created in my head of what might happen were just that: stories. The truth is, I am here today. I am here now. I needed to embrace truth in place of those grim, unsettling stories.

I don't understand why this is happening… and I may never know why. What I *can* do, what I *have to* do, is trust that if God didn't stop this from happening, then this struggle I am experiencing must have purpose.

This book is a compilation of my blog posts and never-before-shared journal writings from the day of my diagnosis with cancer to the end of my treatments. I share these with you because you, or perhaps a loved one, may have something you are struggling with. Cancer or not, please know a struggling heart is a struggling heart. I invite you to join me to…

Pause. Breathe. Pray.

And consider that our struggles have purpose.

I offer for you to think about the caterpillar. A caterpillar wasn't made to be a better caterpillar. It was made to become a butterfly — yet it needs to spend time in its chrysalis to be transformed from a caterpillar into a butterfly.

I see that our struggles are our chrysalis, and our dark times are when we can be transformed into the people we were made to be. Our struggles are there to clear away the clutter of what does not matter in life, to enable us to have clearer perspective and live closer to the heart of what life is all about: to love God and to love others, even in the midst of those struggles.

Through my walk with cancer, as I put that truth into practice, God showed me many life lessons, which I have put together for you here to inspire and encourage you for your walk with _____.

(fill in the blank with your struggle)

No matter our struggles, may we always hold on to hope and trust that *our struggles have purpose.*

With love and hope,
Shawn

P. S. To encourage you, at the end of each chapter I have included a 'Reflection ~ Application Section' where you can reflect on how you can apply the life lesson along your walk with _____.

(your struggle)

LIFE LESSON

1

EMBRACE THE TRUTH RATHER THAN THE STORIES WE CREATE

REFLECTION ~ APPLICATION

Take a moment to...
Pause. Breathe. Pray.

Reflection
♥ Notes to self about this life lesson:

_____

_____

_____

Application
♥ How will you apply this life lesson in your life?

_____

_____

_____

"And you will know the truth, and the truth will set you free"
— John 8:32 (ESV)

DIVINE APPOINTMENTS

Along my walk with cancer, besides the gift of these life lessons, I also experienced many divine appointments.

What is a divine appointment?

Often called a coincidence, serendipitous or fortuitous moments, I believe a divine appointment is when God has placed someone in our path to remind us we are where we need to be and that God is with us on this journey. Throughout these lessons in this book I have interspersed the divine appointments I experienced through my walk with cancer.

These divine appointments have been a blessing to me along the way. They remind me God is with me and wants to walk beside me every day. He uses people, songs and experiences to let me know He is there. Sometimes it just takes clearing away the clutter to see and hear Him. And yes, one gift cancer gave me was to clear away the clutter, allowing me to see and hear God more clearly. I share these gifts throughout this book, to encourage you to realize God is with you too along your walk in life.

I am not unique. I wholeheartedly believe God walks beside each of us every day, through the valleys, along the plateaus, and sits with us on mountaintops, enjoying the views right beside us. I believe He wants to meet each of us exactly where we are and He gifts us with divine appointments along our individual paths in ways that would resonate with who we are and where we are in life to let us know He is there for us.

If you are needing encouragement along your path as well, I invite you to…

Pause. Breathe. Pray.

Let's keep our eyes, ears and heart open to divine appointments along our path. These divine appointments are people, songs, experiences, etc., that will meet us where we are and speak into our hearts in a way that resonates with us. May we be encouraged by these moments as we are reminded that we are where we need to be and God is beside us each step on our individual journeys.

LIFE LESSON

2

YOUR STORY IS NOT ONLINE

When I was told I had stage 3b/4a Adenoid Cystic Carcinoma, ACC, I had no clue what that meant. My doctor graciously informed me it was a rare, slow-growing salivary gland cancer. He explained more details about it, including that it had been around at least a couple of years for the tumor to be the size it was and since it had already eroded bone.

Yep, that wasn't a good thing.

I walked out of that appointment with my head swirling, wanting to know more, but hesitant to look it up online.

Why?

The year before I was diagnosed, my mom had her own walk with cancer. Hers was triple-negative breast cancer. As tough a time as it was to watch my mom undergo surgery, chemotherapy and radiation treatments, she and I both have said her having cancer before me prepared us for my walk with cancer. All our hearts and minds, including my children's, had seen my mom's walk with cancer – and that she was doing well on the other side of treatments. Her story gave us all hope.

Yet when my mom was diagnosed, and while she was undergoing treatments, I refused to look up triple-negative breast cancer. I knew a little about it because it's the type of cancer my best friend's mother had lost her life to. As much as I wanted to know more about this terrible disease, I knew spending my time researching it online would make me more full of fear than faith.

And when my Mom had blood clots in her lungs, I once again chose not to read about them.

Why?

Because the conclusion I came to is my mom's story is not online.

I decided I was going to walk beside her on her journey and live out *her* story with her. I was not going to assume she was going to fall into a certain statistic, because her story was still being lived out.

So when I learned of *my* diagnosis, I was determined not to look it up online.

But… then I did.

Curiosity got the better of me; and yes, I was hoping my online search would provide answers to the many questions I had floating in my mind.

The first page I read online had a number of statistics about ACC and when I got a couple paragraphs in, I closed my computer. Nope, that was not encouraging at all. I sat there on my bed and…

Paused. Breathed. Prayed.

I reminded myself my story is not a part of those statistics. My story is unfinished and only God knows the rest of it. My story is not online.

And yours is not, either.

LIFE LESSON

2

YOUR STORY IS NOT ONLINE

REFLECTION ~ APPLICATION

Take a moment to…
Pause. Breathe. Pray.

Reflection
 ♥ Notes to self about this life lesson:

_____

_____

_____

Application
 ♥ How will you apply this life lesson in your life?

_____

_____

_____

"All the days ordained for me were written in your
book before one of them came to be."
— Psalm 139:16 (NIV)

DIVINE APPOINTMENT

1

As I lay on the stretcher after my biopsy, I was definitely out of it. All I remember was wanting someone to hold my hand. I tried raising my hand to reach out to get someone's attention. I remember trying to say something, but my voice was too faint for anyone to hear me.

Eventually this lovely woman came by to check on me. I asked her to hold my hand. I remember tears streaming down my face because of the comfort of her being there with me. Again, I was a little dazed and don't remember every detail, except she ended up saying a prayer for me. It was such a gift to be there holding her hand and having her pray for me in that delicate moment.

Not every person in that room would have been able to provide me the comfort I needed. Yes, the physical comfort of holding my hand many could do, but this caring woman chose to pray beside me and brought me something I needed in that moment: comfort to my heart, peace to my mind and rest for my soul.

I will be forever grateful for that divine appointment.

KEEP YOUR EYES AND EARS OPEN
FOR **YOUR** NEXT DIVINE APPOINTMENT

LIFE LESSON
3

WE ARE VESSELS FOR LOVE

Cancer came unexpectedly into my world. It invaded my palate and nasal cavity. I have no choice in that. Yet I have a choice whether I will allow cancer to invade my heart, mind and Spirit.

Nope, not today, cancer.

What do I choose to give myself to, if not to cancer?

I choose to give myself to God, my husband, my children, my family, my friends, my community.

I choose to give myself to love, to kindness, to compassion, to patience, to perseverance, to forgiveness, to mercy, to grace.

I choose to give myself to hope.

I may have cancer in my body but cancer will never invade my Spirit.

I will be practicing letting go and trusting God through this journey. I am grateful the waves of peace have outweighed the waves of sadness and fear recently.

My hope is to heal completely and be off this road soon; yet I trust, whatever the outcome, all will be well for me, and for those I love, because God can make good of all things – even cancer.

It will be easier said than done, depending on the moment. I know in my heart my body was created to be a vessel for love – and I refuse to allow cancer to stop me from living out love throughout my days.

I invite you to join me to...

Pause. Breathe. Pray.

And let's choose to align our bodies with their divine purpose: to be vessels for love.

Let's choose to focus our minds and meditate on words that will nourish our souls.

Let's choose to focus our eyes on the good in ourselves, in others and in the world and look only one step ahead at a time.

Let's choose to tune our ears in to divine wisdom and guidance and follow where it leads.

Let's choose to use silence as an expression of love so we may listen to people's hearts when they speak. Also, when we choose to speak, let's speak the truth in love, building others up and encouraging them to be the people God made them to be.

Let's choose to use our arms to carry each other's burdens, use our hands to extend the offer of friendship to others and bless others who have a need around us.

Let's choose to use our legs to stand up for what is right, even when it is hard.

Let's choose to use our feet to walk the path of peace, inviting others beside us on the journey.

May we remember we may not be able to control what happens to our bodies, but we are able to choose to use it as a vessel of love, no matter our circumstances, today and always.

LIFE LESSON

3

WE ARE VESSELS FOR LOVE

REFLECTION ~ APPLICATION

Take a moment to…
Pause. Breathe. Pray.

Reflection
♥ Notes to self about this life lesson:

_____

_____

_____

Application
♥ How will you apply this life lesson in your life?

_____

_____

_____

"Do everything in love."
– Corinthians 16:14 (NIV)

LIFE LESSON

4

HOPE ANCHORS THE SOUL

As I walked from appointment to appointment on my first visit to Boston, there was an awful tension forming in my neck and shoulders. This was odd because, with my history of anxiety and depression, I was surprised I had yet to have a panic attack or experience all the anxiety I used to. Rather than my internal world carrying the tension of all I was experiencing, it appeared my body took on that tension.

I sat in the examination chair at the oncologist's office. The resident doctor met with me before the oncologist came in. He started asking me questions, but the throbbing, intense pain in my neck and shoulders was growing worse and worse; and, as much as I tried, I could not find a comfortable position that would allow me to tune in to what he was saying.

The resident was compassionate and paused the conversation to try to help me get more comfortable before going on.

What I realized in that moment was my body was holding on to all the tension I was carrying from my diagnosis. I literally couldn't move my head in any direction more than a quarter of an inch without the pain increasing. And the throbbing was like a migraine multiplied a hundredfold. The tension was absolutely debilitating.

This wasn't going to work. I needed to hold onto something else to get through this.

I recognized that every day we hold on to something. Maybe it's tension, worry, fear, anger, sadness, etc. Yet is what we are holding on to helping us, or harming us?

If you, too, are holding on to something that is inhibiting you from being the vessel of love you were made to be, I invite you to join me to…

Pause. Breathe. Pray.

And may we lay down what is weighing us down. In place of it, let's choose to hold on to something that will lift us up instead, let's hold on to hope.

When I chose to hold on to hope and lay down the rest (through prayer, soothing salt baths, heat packs and acupuncture), hope helped anchor my soul and birth the possibility that all will be well, in time.

That sounds nice, but what does it mean?

One night as I rested in the warm bath with my lavender candle flickering beside me, I had a heart to heart with God. I told God all my hopes and dreams and if he had more for me to do here, I'm ready to do it; but if I've done all that was mine to do, I asked him to prepare my heart to go home to heaven to heal.

You see, the hope I was focused on was to get my way of being healed. And yes, I wanted my way, to be healed and free of cancer, moving on and experiencing life with Stephen, Kate, Gavin and Matthew for many years to come. But there is another hope I opened my eyes to: the hope of going to heaven to heal.

And it was in those moments of seeing both outcomes – and trusting all would be well, in time, no matter the outcome – hope truly anchored my soul.

Whatever struggle is on our heart, may we let go of all that is causing us unnecessary tension, in mind or body. May we instead hold on to hope and trust that all will be well in God's time. May hope anchor our soul, and give us peace within, no matter our circumstances.

LIFE LESSON
4
HOPE ANCHORS THE SOUL

REFLECTION ~ APPLICATION

Take a moment to…
Pause. Breathe. Pray.

Reflection
 ♥ Notes to self about this life lesson:

_____

_____

_____

Application
 ♥ How will you apply this life lesson in your life?

_____

_____

_____

"We have this hope as an anchor for the soul."
— Hebrews 6:19 (NIV)

LIFE LESSON

5

THE WORLD NEEDS YOUR LIGHT

Yesterday I read a story* about a man whose house lost power at night. He went to light candles for his family so they could see better and not have to navigate their way through their house in the dark. When he went to light the candles, they started speaking to him. The candles had excuses as to why they were not ready to be lit and chose to remain unlit, not providing light to the man and his family while they were in the dark.

When I looked up from this story, I saw two candles that have sat on a shelf in our home for the 12 years we have been married. We have never placed them on the table or used them; they have never been used for their intended purpose.

I thought, "How many of us are unlit candles, having yet to put our purpose into action in this life?"

Having cancer makes me realize tomorrow is never promised, cancer or not. I don't want to get to the end of my life having not lit my candle and shared with the world what is mine to share for God. Whatever our struggle, let us be reminded there is a light inside each of us waiting to be lit and shine light into the darkness, a light only we can offer.

Today I offer for each of us to…

Pause. Breathe. Pray.

Just as the man needed the candles to light his home, the world needs us to light our candle within, align with our God-given purpose in life, and put it into action to bring light into the world, even in the midst of our struggles.

Let us not allow our current circumstances to weigh us down. Instead, let us choose to be a light in the darkness and let our inner light shine today. May we brighten our space in this world, in our homes, in our communities and beyond.

May we choose to let our light shine until we are at the end of our wick.

*The story referenced above is from the book, *God Came Near*, by Max Lucado, 2013, Nashville, TN, Thomas Nelson

LIFE LESSON

5

THE WORLD NEEDS YOUR LIGHT

REFLECTION ~ APPLICATION

Take a moment to…
Pause. Breathe. Pray.

Reflection
♥ Notes to self about this life lesson:

_____

_____

_____

Application
♥ How will you apply this life lesson in your life?

_____

_____

_____

"Let your light shine before others."
— Matthew 5:16 (NIV)

LIFE LESSON

6

THE WIND HELPS TREES GROW DEEPER ROOTS

Years ago I heard a story about a group of researchers who attempted to grow trees indoors. Initially, the trees grew, but at some point they all broke. The researchers came to the conclusion they had left out a critical component to help the trees thrive: *wind.* They realized the wind actually helped the trees grow stronger.

This story parallels our struggles, which are there to strengthen us, from the inside out.

Yes, branches fall off trees while the wind blows, but those are the weak parts of the tree inhibiting it from growing into its strongest expression of itself.

The same is true for us.

May our struggles help prune us of the things that inhibit us from growing into the best version of ourselves... the fear, the worry, the anger, the frustration. May our trials prune those things from our hearts and minds so we can gain perspective on the beauty of the day in front of us and our purpose here: to love God (and if that doesn't resonate with you, to love love) and to live out love toward others.

It sounds simple, but the practice of this can be challenging. But as I sit here watching the wind blow through the trees, and knowing they are growing stronger I am...

Pausing. Breathing. Praying.

In hopes I can see my walk with cancer as the wind, meant to deepen my roots of faith and help me grow more into the person God made me to be.

I pray you can see your walk with _____ in the same way.   (your struggle)

LIFE LESSON

6

THE WIND HELPS TREES GROW DEEPER ROOTS

REFLECTION ~ APPLICATION

Take a moment to…

Pause. Breathe. Pray.

Reflection
♥ Notes to self about this life lesson:

_____

_____

_____

Application
♥ How will you apply this life lesson in your life?

_____

_____

_____

"Blessed is the one who perseveres under trial because,
having stood the test, that person will receive the crown of life
that God has promised to those who love him."
— James 1:12 (NIV)

LIFE LESSON

7

GOD IS THE EYE OF THE STORM

My mind is messy. The stories some days are louder than the truth, so I need to infuse truth into my heart and mind often.

Music has been a godsend.

I've been growing my playlist with encouraging songs that fuel my soul. Songs like, "Oceans" by Hillsong United, "Trust In You" by Lauren Daigle, "Cast My Cares" by Finding Favour, "Strong Enough" by Matthew West and "Riser" by Dierks Bentley.

One song that has captured my heart is "Eye of the Storm" by Ryan Stevenson. As the thoughts swirl around with the unknown of what is to come, I have a choice to get wrapped up in this hurricane of thoughts and emotions, or I can go to God, who is the eye of the storm, where there is peace, calm, comfort and safety.

I am doing my best to fight the story-filled winds that are trying to carry me away into the chaos and instead sit with God in the eye of this storm.

As the lyrics read:

When the solid ground is falling out from underneath my feet
Between the black skies, and my red eyes, I can barely see...
When my hopes and dreams are far from me
And I'm running out of faith
I see the future I picture slowly fade away
And when the tears of pain and heartache
Are pouring down my face

I find my peace in Jesus' name
In the eye of the storm
You remain in control
And in the middle of the war
You guard my soul
You alone are the anchor
When my sails are torn
Your love surrounds me
In the eye of the storm

And the song concludes with my favorite Psalm...

The Lord is my Shepherd
I have all that I need
He lets me rest in green meadows
He leads me beside peaceful streams
He renews my strength
He guides me along right paths, bringing honor to His Name
Even when I walk through the darkest valley, I will not be afraid
For You are close beside me.

- Psalm 23 (NLT).

The words in this song speak deep into my heart, reminding me God wants me to have peace of mind, even with cancer. And He wants the same for you too. If you also find yourself wrapped up in the hurricane of stories in your mind around your struggle, I invite you to join me to...

Pause. Breathe. Pray.

And consider stepping into the eye of the storm with me to help us through this hurricane season. God is always waiting for us there, to be our refuge and strength in our times of struggle.

LIFE LESSON

7

GOD IS THE EYE OF THE STORM

REFLECTION ~ APPLICATION

Take a moment to…
Pause. Breathe. Pray.

Reflection
 ♥ Notes to self about this life lesson:

_____

_____

_____

Application
 ♥ How will you apply this life lesson in your life?

_____

_____

_____

"God is our refuge and strength,
an ever-present help in trouble."
— Psalm 46:1(NIV)

LIFE LESSON

8

BE KIND TO OTHERS
(EVEN WHEN THEY MAY NOT DESERVE IT)

I went to the cardiologist to get clearance for my upcoming surgery. While I was waiting to check in, the elderly woman in front of me was sharing with the secretary many of her ailments. At the end, she said she just had a scan and was happy it wasn't cancer.

I thought how fortunate she was to receive that diagnosis. I unfortunately don't have the luxury to utter those words.

She sat down. I checked in. Then, on my way to my seat, I smiled at her.

She huffed, "What are you smiling at?" in my direction.

Before you judge this woman, listen to what came next.

Having heard her complain about her ailments and then be so quick to dismiss a kind gesture, I knew this woman needed someone to listen to her, not someone to judge her. I asked if she was okay with my sitting next to her.

Once again she grumbled her response. "If you want to."

You may think I'm crazy for giving this woman my time and attention, especially after how she treated me. Yet, what I learned as a teacher was the students who were most challenging needed love, not judgment. Often when I gave them an open ear and my time, they would let me in behind the mask they wore. I find the same is true as a Mom.

I am finding the same is true with adults.

So I sat and listened to her story. Every statement was negative and it was as though she felt the world was against her. You can see how many people observing her from the outside in would say she was a grumpy old woman. Yet, by listening to her, I had the chance to meet her from the inside out and see she was a woman, a widow, a mother, whose many ailments were challenging her in mind, body and spirit. For those minutes I sat with her, I listened and I got to step out of myself and my situation to be there for her. By the end, she was in tears and we were hugging.

I am sure many people may think I had every right to be annoyed with this woman and could have just brushed her off... yet that is what is happening too much in society. We may think our issues or stories are more significant than others' and therefore we walk around focused on ourselves rather than taking the opportunities that arise to step outside of ourselves to practice being present and kind to others.

For me, engaging with this woman and meeting her behind her shell, where her truth resides, broadened my heart that day. She has been in my thoughts and prayers since. Being able to wish her well – even if she never knows it, is a gift I carry in my heart daily, especially during this time.

I share this story in hopes the next time we meet someone, young, old, or somewhere in between, with a hard shell, we are able to...

Pause. Breathe. Pray.

And see beyond the surface, into their heart where their truth resides. May we choose to step out of our circumstances momentarily and show up for them. May we be kind, even if they do not deserve it. May we choose to bridge hearts with them fueling our soul, and theirs, in the process. It may not be the easier choice, but it will be the worthwhile one.

LIFE LESSON
8

BE KIND TO OTHERS
(EVEN WHEN THEY MAY NOT DESERVE IT)

<u>REFLECTION ~ APPLICATION</u>

Take a moment to...
Pause. Breathe. Pray.

<u>Reflection</u>
♥ Notes to self about this life lesson:

_____

_____

_____

<u>Application</u>
♥ How will you apply this life lesson in your life?

_____

_____

_____

"Be kind and compassionate to one another,
forgiving each other, just as God forgave you."
– Ephesians 4:32 (NIV)

LIFE LESSON

9

YOU ARE ENCIRCLED WITH LOVE

As I lie in bed at night, many nights that is where my tears flow. Sometimes because of the fear of the unknown, sometimes it's the sadness of what is to come with my upcoming surgery and time away from my family. I know what I am going through is a lot to process, and it is there, in the quiet safety and comfort of my bed, I let the emotions flow.

Yet what has been a gift to me as I lay my head down at night – or at my appointments and during all the scans, MRIs and other tests and procedures – are the people around us right now.

As I lie, or sit, I…

Pause. Breathe. Pray.

And I picture the circles of love wrapped around our family.

The first circle around us is God. Then around me are my husband and children. Next come our parents, who are then surrounded by our siblings, their spouses and our nieces and nephews. The next circle of love around us is our extended family. The next circles are our caring friends, then our thoughtful community.

Every circle of love makes my heart smile and provides me with comfort, strength, peace and hope for the journey ahead.

I am sharing this for wherever you are in your struggle. Although often we may be alone, whether in our home, waiting in a doctor's office, etc., may we never forget there are people who love us.

I invite you to join me to…

Pause. Breathe. Pray.

And take a moment to draw the circles of love that exist around you. Whether they be small or large, may they be mighty and make your heart smile, giving you comfort, strength, peace and hope for your journey, too.

LIFE LESSON

9

YOU ARE ENCIRCLED WITH LOVE

REFLECTION ~ APPLICATION

Take a moment to…
Pause. Breathe. Pray.

Reflection
♥ Notes to self about this life lesson:

_____

_____

_____

Application
♥ How will you apply this life lesson in your life?

_____

_____

_____

"Be devoted to one another in love.
Honor one another above yourselves."
– Romans 12:10 (NIV)

LIFE LESSON

10

BAD NEWS BRINGS PERSPECTIVE

Today I was driving to the dentist with two of my children. My third child had gone last week, where they learned of their first cavities. As we were driving today, one of my children said, "Ever since I heard that [my sibling] has cavities, I have been brushing much better."

After complimenting them on their newfound accomplishment (of finally doing what they were supposed to be doing all along), I laughed on the inside.

I realized often it takes hearing bad news to bring perspective. Bad news gives us momentum to start doing things we always knew we needed to do – or to do them more efficiently.

In my current circumstances, from the moment I heard I have cancer, suddenly I've seen life more clearly. So many of the little things that really don't matter in life have fallen away, leaving what matters most: my faith and my family. In our family, the little arguments seem to have faded as well.

It's like when someone passes away, you suddenly see the brevity of life and want to live life fully and completely, close to what matters most. Yet then time passes, and you slowly go back into your old patterns, losing perspective.

I invite you to join me to…

Pause. Breathe. Pray.

If we have been given bad news, may it give us sight to see life clearly. And if you haven't received bad news, please don't wait for it to come your way to give you perspective in life and bring you close to what matters most. Let's each choose to live that way today!

LIFE LESSON
10
BAD NEWS BRINGS PERSPECTIVE

REFLECTION ~ APPLICATION

Take a moment to…
Pause. Breathe. Pray.

Reflection
♥ Notes to self about this life lesson:

_____

_____

_____

Application
♥ How will you apply this life lesson in your life?

_____

_____

_____

"They will have no fear of bad news,
their hearts are steadfast, trusting in God."
— Psalm 112:7 (NIV)

LIFE LESSON

11

RECEIVE GIFTS FROM OTHERS
WITH A GRATEFUL HEART

We had dinner with my parents, my sisters and their families the other day. You could also have called this gathering an intervention.

You see, Stephen and I are givers and doers. We've been moving through our day-to-day routines not seeking help from others unless it was absolutely needed. For example, if we had an appointment and our kids needed to be picked up and cared for, we have been fine asking for help.

Yet, when people started offering to bring us meals, do our laundry, clean our home, etc., it has been uncomfortable for us to receive those, because they weren't what we considered needs. We are surrounded by such amazing family, friends and community, we are being blessed daily with offers for people to help in any way they can.

The thing is, we are still able to do these things, and therefore didn't see a need for others to help us. But, as my sisters pointed out, by our saying no to people from helping, we're not allowing them to love on us.

Hmm... that got me thinking from a new angle. Yes, Stephen and I didn't *need* the help... yet. We knew after the surgery and during my treatments, we would have to lean on people more to help with the kids and carpooling, etc. We really didn't want to ask until there was a need.

Yet, there was a need – but it wasn't ours.

Our family and friends needed to express love to us for their own hearts to have more peace. We had never considered it from that angle before, but I know if I was the one wanting to love on someone else and lighten their load, it would warm my heart to be able to do so.

So we waved the white flag and surrendered to receive, even though it felt extremely uncomfortable for us.

The love that flowed our way was so thoughtful and generous. We received every loving word and act of love with grateful hearts.

If you are a giver and doer and have trouble receiving, like we do, I invite you to join me to…

Pause. Breathe. Pray.

May we remember that love blesses the giver and the receiver. May we be willing to get out of our own way so others can be the vessel of love they were called to be, and may we receive loving gifts from others with grateful hearts.

LIFE LESSON
11

RECEIVE GIFTS FROM OTHERS
WITH A GRATEFUL HEART

REFLECTION ~ APPLICATION

Take a moment to…
Pause. Breathe. Pray.

Reflection
♥ Notes to self about this life lesson:

_____

_____

_____

Application
♥ How will you apply this life lesson in your life?

_____

_____

_____

"Give thanks in all circumstances, for this is God's will for you."
— 1 Thessalonians 5:18 (NIV)

LIFE LESSON

12

TRUST THE PROCESS

I love to bake with my kids. One of my kids is in charge of muffin making, another biscuits, and the third makes the family pizza dough on Fridays.

To each of those recipes there is a process. If you miss a step or an ingredient in the muffins, biscuits or pizza dough, or try to rush the process, they won't turn out how they are meant to be.

A dear friend shared with me once that it is significant to 'trust the process.' I think and say that often.

When things feel messy, and the uncertainty of what is ahead comes to the surface, I need to...

Pause. Breathe. Pray.

This walk with cancer is a process that will take time for me to move through, yet I need to go step by step, trusting the process. I need the surgery. I then need to heal from that. I will need to adjust to my new mouth. I will need radiation and chemotherapy. I will then need time to heal from those too. I need to look at each of these steps as ingredients to my healing and trust that God is baking up something beautiful on the other side of all of this.

Whatever your struggle may be, I invite you to join me to...

Pause. Breathe. Pray.

May we not rush through the process but walk step by step through it, trusting each step is needed for the outcome to be what God needs to be.

LIFE LESSON
12
TRUST THE PROCESS

REFLECTION ~ APPLICATION

Take a moment to…
Pause. Breathe. Pray.

Reflection
♥ Notes to self about this life lesson:

_____

_____

_____

Application
♥ How will you apply this life lesson in your life?

_____

_____

_____

"Trust in God with all your heart and lean not on your own understanding.
In all your ways acknowledge him and He will make your path straight."
— Proverbs 3:5-6 (ESV)

LIFE LESSON

13

THE HARD TIMES
REFINE THE DIAMOND

For my birthday last November, Stephen surprised me with a trip to Nashville. We had always wanted to go there together, and I was so excited to finally go!

The trip was scheduled for January, and it included tickets to a Dierks Bentley concert. We are country music fans and Dierks happened to be playing the weekend we were going. While we were at the concert that Saturday night in Nashville at the Bridgestone Arena, Dierks moved from the main stage and came to the back to a small stage right in front of us. I can't remember whether he played more than one song, but the one that has stayed with me is titled "Riser."

This song breathes life into the dark spaces in my mind. While Mom was going through her walk with breast cancer, it was a song I listened to often. I had also shared it with Mom to remind her she was a Riser, a fighter, a survivor.

I taped the song that night at the concert, with tears of gratitude rolling down my face that Mom is doing well. When the song ended, I texted Mom the song, so full of joy, grateful there are encouraging songs that support people in their time of need.

That was Saturday, January 21st.

We arrived home from Nashville Tuesday, January 24th.

The doctor found my tumor Wednesday, January 25th.

I replay that moment at the concert in my head and thank God for reminding me of such a beautiful message of hope days before I was diagnosed. This song is now one of my go-to songs to encourage me as I walk this journey with cancer.

I am a Riser.

I rise every morning to grow in a deeper relationship with God.

I rise every day hopeful to be the wife Stephen needs to grow into his best self.

I rise every day hopeful to be the mom to Kate, Gavin and Matthew who encourages and supports them to grow into the people God made them to be.

I rise every day hopeful to live out love to my friends, within my community and to strangers I meet along the way.

Yes, cancer is part of my journey and it could weigh me down – as it does at times – but it is in those moments I need to choose to be a riser, and rise above the waves and look at the horizon, full of beauty and light… at the day ahead of me.

Yes, my cancer is real, it is invasive, its path and my long-term future are unknown. But as the Dierks Bentley song goes:

"The hard times put the shine into the diamond."

This is a hard time but it is one that is meant not to break me, but to refine me. I see it as a purification process for my heart, mind and soul. I am practicing letting go of the little things and focusing more on God and being the person He made me to be, a vessel of love.

I am a riser… cancer cannot keep down my desire to share messages of hope, encouragement and love. I won't let it.

You also may be dealing with something. Maybe it isn't cancer, but it is still significant in your life. I encourage you to join me to…

Pause. Breathe. Pray.

Let's choose to each be a riser and let the hard times refine us, rubbing away all that is insignificant in our lives, giving us brilliant clarity as to who and what matter in life; God and people. And may the refining process also reveal the radiant diamond we were each made to be. Shine bright, friend! The world needs your light.

LIFE LESSON
13
THE HARD TIMES
REFINE THE DIAMOND

REFLECTION ~ APPLICATION

Take a moment to…
Pause. Breathe. Pray.

Reflection
♥ Notes to self about this life lesson:

_____

_____

_____

Application
♥ How will you apply this life lesson in your life?

_____

_____

_____

"Though you may have had to endure many trials, these trials will
show that your faith is genuine. It is being tested as fire tests and
purifies gold, though your faith is far more precious than mere gold."
— 1 Peter 1:6-7 (NIV)

LIFE LESSON

14

GOD GIVES US TOOLS
FOR THE TRIALS

We arrived a day early in Boston the night before my maxillectomy surgery, because of an expected snowstorm headed our way. We filled our day with joy and laughter. Stephen and I even walked to and from the hospital as the snow fell, to see how long a walk it was. I would be staying at this hotel during my radiation and chemo treatments for seven weeks and I planned to walk to and from my daily treatments.

Stephen, my mom, dad and I were in my parents' hotel room, playing a board game, when suddenly a wave of fear washed over me.

Will I survive? What will I look like? And what will I sound like after my palate is removed?

The uncertainty of what the following day held brought a numbness over me. I gave Stephen a look and he knew I needed to retreat to our room. We left my parents' room and went back to ours, where I numbed out, watching HGTV and stuffing popcorn into my mouth, since I wasn't sure when I would be able to eat it again.

Stephen tapped me on the arm and showed me that he was receiving texts from our family and friends, including a few that had videos. As we read the texts and watched the videos, they brought so much warmth to my heart. When we finished watching the last video, reality sunk in and my heart was gripped by fear again.

I scrolled through my phone, searching for a picture of a poem a friend had given me. I was seeking peace for my heart and mind in the midst of all this uncertainty.

I found the poem and read it over and over again…

> *God hath not promised skies always blue,*
> *Flower strewn pathways all our lives through,*
> *God hath not promised sun without rain,*
> *Joy without sorrow, peace without pain.*
> *But God hath promised strength for the day,*
> *Rest for the labor, light for the way,*
> *Grace for the trials, help from above,*
> *Unfailing sympathy, undying love.*
> *– Annie Johnson Flint*

The truth in these words flooded my heart. This life was not meant to be trouble free. I am meant to look to God in the trials to provide me with the tools I need to get me through this time.

I will not say fear left me that night, because I would be lying. But I will say holding on to the truth that God will provide me with the tools I need to get through the trial allowed me to sleep that night.

Whatever your trials may be, I invite you to join me to…
Pause. Breathe. Pray.

And may we remember this life is not meant to be without trials. Yet, our trials are meant to remind us God is there, ready with the tools we need to help us get through.

He is waiting to give them to us. All we have to do is ask.

LIFE LESSON
14
GOD GIVES US TOOLS
FOR THE TRIALS

REFLECTION ~ APPLICATION

Take a moment to…
Pause. Breathe. Pray.

Reflection
♥ Notes to self about this life lesson:

_____

_____

_____

Application
♥ How will you apply this life lesson in your life?

_____

_____

_____

"Be joyful in hope, patient in affliction, faithful in prayer."
— Romans 12:12 (NIV)

DIVINE APPOINTMENT

2

The day of my maxillectomy surgery arrived and, as expected, I was a little unnerved. The meds I received prior to going into the operating room put me in a deeply relaxed state. A couple of people came to wheel me in to the operating room. As I let go of Stephen's hand, I was placed into the hands of people I didn't know.

The woman kindly introduced herself, then proceeded to introduce the gentleman with her. For some reason she shared with me that he was a spiritual person. I introduced myself to him and shared that spirituality is important to me, too. This compassionate gentleman chose to speak faith-filled words of encouragement into my heart on our walk into the operating room. It was a brief encounter, but one that will always stay with me.

This gentleman could have just pushed another person into surgery, yet he chose to engage with me and share his loving heart with me in a moment when I needed it. His words brought me peace as I was wheeled into the operating room, and reminded me God is with me and, although I cannot see him, He is using people beside me along my walk to be a vessel for His love towards me.

KEEP YOUR EYES AND EARS OPEN
FOR **YOUR** NEXT DIVINE APPOINTMENT

DIVINE APPOINTMENT

3

When I arrived in the operating room in a drug-induced, drowsy state, I asked those in the room to come by my side as I wanted to thank them for being there to care for me that day. I honestly don't know what I said, if anything, because the meds kicked in big time. The only thing I do remember was this beautiful voice whispering in my ear, "Jesus is with you. Jesus loves you." The sweet voice repeated this comforting truth to me a few times before the medicine sent me into the deep sleep for surgery.

Before I go on, I want to say that hearing "Jesus" can make some people cringe and others smile. Please know I used to be someone who would hear "Jesus" and think, "Okay, good for you, but that's not my thing." Through my last journey with anxiety and depression, I came back to my faith and, in doing so, have a new view when I hear Jesus' name. Please know I am sharing this moment with you not to impose my spiritual path on you but to share that God met me where I am spiritually in this divine appointment and used this beautiful soul to speak words that would bring peace to my heart and mind in a particularly tumultuous moment.

I wholeheartedly believe God speaks to all of us – yet in ways that resonate with where we are on our spiritual walk.

That said, I admit I wondered afterward whether I had dreamt the whole thing. It seemed a little too perfectly aligned to have been true. Yet while I was in the hospital, healing, I met the young woman with the sweet voice who soothed my soul and I got to thank her for blessing me with the divine appointment in the operating room that day. What a gift she was to me! I will always carry her in my heart.

KEEP YOUR EYES AND EARS OPEN
FOR **YOUR** NEXT DIVINE APPOINTMENT

LIFE LESSON
15

BRIDGE HEARTS WITH OTHERS

I woke up in a drug-induced fog, unable to speak with my tongue and face swollen from surgery. As I lay there, I found comfort in seeing Stephen beside me. (What a gift that he has always been there beside me.) As my parents, sisters and best friend visited, I wasn't able to communicate well and resorted to answering using a thumbs up as needed.

Somewhere in that first 24 hours as I went to sit up, I felt the new roof of my mouth, my obturator (think glorified retainer), fall onto my tongue. It had been screwed in to the top of what was left of my palate behind my front teeth, and hooked onto a couple of my teeth, but obviously it didn't hold well. I looked at Stephen, pointing at my mouth, moaning, hoping he'd see what I was talking about. In his calm way, he let me know he heard me and proceeded to be sure I got the help I needed, which included going to see my obturator guy. (I know there is a more sophisticated name for him, but that is my formal name for him.)

As I was wheeled down the white hospital hallway, we turned a corner into this small room, where I was placed in a dentist's chair with the dental light shining in my eyes so bright it was hard to keep them open.

Stephen stood beside me, holding my hand as the doctor worked the obturator back in place. Now that may sound easy, but I had just had my palate, my back three upper teeth and their gums

71

removed. My mouth was raw, swollen and sensitive, with exposed nerves. Every movement the doctor made included pressing the obturator up against my newly created wounds. It was like stubbing your toe on the corner of the door when your toe is already cut open… or maybe more like all ten toes at once. Let's just say the word painful is an understatement.

Stephen was beside me as I gave birth naturally to our three children. In all those experiences combined he said he never heard me cry out in pain like I did that day. Tears flowed as I thought there was no hope of an end to this excruciating pain I was experiencing. Poor Stephen wanted to punch the guy for the pain he was causing me – which is extremely uncharacteristic of him, yet explains the intensity of our experience.

The doctor was able to get the obturator back in. I left there crying – I am not sure whether it was because I was still in pain or relieved that it was over. I went back to my bed shaking from all I had just experienced, took meds to help the pain and, with Stephen still beside me, I dozed off to sleep.

And the next day it happened again.

I looked at Stephen and with tears of fear in my eyes bluntly told him, in my new mumbled voice, "I am not going back." I went the first week with my obturator not fully in place so my mouth would have time to heal before having my doctor put it in place again.

I knew my doctor was doing his job, yet in that raw moment I wanted him to see beyond my mouth and look into my hurting heart. Since that day, I have gotten to know, love and trust my obturator guy. (*First impressions can be deceiving.*) Yet the lesson I learned that day is significant in life.

Every day we interact with others. Often we see the body but how often do we look beyond the surface and seek to bridge hearts with the other person? Whatever we do, whether we are a spouse, a parent, a doctor, cashier, mailman, chef, secretary, garbage man, teacher, etc. May we stop going through the motions and become present with one another. Let's take a moment to…

Pause. Breathe. Pray.

And let's look beyond the surface of the body and into the heart of the people we interact with. Let's be each other's life guards and be intentional *and* directional with what we say and/or do so we can bridge hearts and truly connect with one another.

LIFE LESSON
15
BRIDGE HEARTS WITH OTHERS

REFLECTION ~ APPLICATION

Take a moment to…
Pause. Breathe. Pray.

Reflection
♥ Notes to self about this life lesson:

_____

_____

_____

Application
♥ How will you apply this life lesson in your life?

_____

_____

_____

"People look at the outward appearance,
God looks at the heart."
– 1 Samuel 16:7 (NIV)

LIFE LESSON

16

CHOOSE TO LOVE, NOT JUDGE

I felt raw yesterday, physically and emotionally. I went back for my post-op appointment, which included having my obturator adjusted. Getting it adjusted was uncomfortable, but it went better than I anticipated, thankfully.

Although it was manageable, I was still left feeling raw – not just physically, but emotionally.

Why?

Prior to my appointment, I had an interaction with someone that left me realizing my life has changed.

As Stephen and I sat down to wait for our appointment, I smiled at the man near us, as I would have two weeks ago without my obturator, and got a smile in return. Then I followed it with, "How are you doing today?"

When I saw his blank stare in response, and noted how his eyes darted away from mine, avoiding interacting with me, it took me a moment to realize I'd forgotten I sound different these days. While adjusting to the obturator, I sounded like a cross between Charlie Brown's teacher and the person taking your order at a fast-food drive thru.

I realized my voice made him uncomfortable and, rather than engaging in a conversation with me, he chose to avoid me.

My heart broke.

Not for me so much – although it was disheartening for a moment, realizing I was being judged for my voice. I was surprised at how quickly the smile he'd worn on his face just moments before disappeared. For me, my voice is temporary as I adjust to my new mouth and, in time, I hope to speak clearly again.

What I was heartbroken about was how many people – children and adults alike – walk through life every day with visible/audible deformities and others judge them and pretend they don't exist.

I got a taste of it yesterday and what it did for me was wake me up to be sure I engage with people – no matter what they look like or sound like – because they are human beings and deserve to be recognized.

Imagine how many beautiful souls are passed by, simply because people lack knowledge and understanding, and therefore label someone as different and unworthy of their time.

So I leave you with this thought: Next time you see someone who may look different or talk differently, etc., I ask that you...

Pause. Breathe. Pray.

Take a moment to put yourself in their shoes and ask yourself, "How would I like someone treating me if that was me?"

My hope is that all of us would choose to interact with that person and treat them with kindness, dignity and respect and let them know they are seen and heard.

In place of judgment, let's choose to love one another.

LIFE LESSON

16

CHOOSE TO LOVE, NOT JUDGE

REFLECTION ~ APPLICATION

Take a moment to…
Pause. Breathe. Pray.

Reflection
♥ Notes to self about this life lesson:

_____

_____

_____

Application
♥ How will you apply this life lesson in your life?

_____

_____

_____

"Love your neighbors as yourself."
— Leviticus 19:18 (NIV)

LIFE LESSON

17

WEAR THE LENS OF GRATITUDE

I am physically deformed. No one can see it but me. But every morning and night I take out my obturator and see that hole in my mouth. It is something I will see every morning and night for the rest of my life.

Every time I go to swallow, I am learning how my new mouth works and do my best not to send the liquids I sip down the wrong pipe or have it exit my nose.

This is my new reality since my surgery.

Yet I am seeing that every day *I have a choice* in how I view my deformity, my obturator, my routines, my new reality.

I can choose to be frustrated with it or grateful for it.

I can choose to be frustrated at needing to use a syringe as a utensil to feed myself, or be grateful a syringe is available as a utensil for me to use.

I can choose to be frustrated with my morning and night routine that can last 45 minutes each, or be grateful we have things like sinus cleanses and salt & baking-soda washes that aid the healing process.

I can choose to be frustrated with the fact I have an obturator and I sound different, or I can be grateful devices accessible to me – like the obturator – give me the ability to speak.

I choose to be grateful. Do I stray from that at times? Absolutely. But it is the truth I promise myself I will continue returning to until it becomes a habit.

How we see things matters.

I invite you to take a moment to think about something you are frustrated with. Then join me to take a moment to…

Pause. Breathe. Pray.

Let's see if we can shift from being frustrated to being grateful. For the lens we wear today gives us the perspective through which we see things.

Let's choose the lens of gratitude, because through this lens, we will receive more peace within our hearts and minds.

LIFE LESSON
17
WEAR THE LENS OF GRATITUDE

REFLECTION ~ APPLICATION

Take a moment to…
Pause. Breathe. Pray.

Reflection
♥ Notes to self about this life lesson:

_____

_____

_____

Application
♥ How will you apply this life lesson in your life?

_____

_____

_____

"Do not be anxious about anything, but in every situation, by prayer and petition, with thanksgiving, present your requests to God."
— Philippians 4:6 (NIV)

LIFE LESSON

18

A SEED NEEDS TO BREAK
IN ORDER TO GROW
(AND SO MAY YOU)

As I heal, it is a blessing to do things at home that are part of our normal routine. One of those things for us is every spring for the past number of years, my kids and I plant seeds indoors and care for them until we are able to plant them outside in our community garden. Planting the seeds with my kids was therapeutic for me in many ways.

As we have watched the seeds begin to sprout, I am reminded these seeds needed to break in the soil in order to begin to grow into these sprouts.

It made me think: I am like these seeds buried in the darkness of cancer.

Yet like these seeds, what if my body being broken means something new is coming? Just like the sprouts came from the broken seed, maybe something beautiful will bloom this experience, in its time.

With these seeds, the packets tell us what will grow; unfortunately only God knows what He will grow from this experience. Just as these seeds rest in the soil, my hope is to rest too in faith, trusting that God will create something beautiful out of this experience. And like the seeds that will sprout into flowers and food that will nourish others, I hope whatever comes from this, God will use to nourish others, too.

And if you also are in a dark place, I invite you to see this isn't the end, but rather the start of something new blooming in your life.

I invite you to join me to…

Pause. Breathe. Pray.

And may we view our struggles as a time of transformation, breaking us free of the old shell and sprouting into something new.

May we allow God's truth to be the water and His love to be the sunlight, as we allow this dark season to be a transformative time during which we unfold into the people we were made to be.

LIFE LESSON
18

A SEED NEEDS TO BREAK
IN ORDER TO GROW
(AND SO MAY YOU)

REFLECTION ~ APPLICATION

Take a moment to...
Pause. Breathe. Pray.

Reflection
♥ Notes to self about this life lesson:

_____

_____

_____

Application
♥ How will you apply this life lesson in your life?

_____

_____

_____

"Forget the former things; do not dwell on the past.
See, I am doing a new thing! I am making a way in the
wilderness and streams in the wasteland."
-- Isaiah 43:18-19 (NIV)

LIFE LESSON

19

OUR DAYS ARE NUMBERED; USE THEM WISELY

In a random act of nature, one of our local school bus drivers lost his life due to a tree falling on the bus this week. Though I sit here uncertain of what my future holds with cancer, the truth is, cancer or not, tomorrow is never guaranteed.

And all that keeps popping into my head is: Life is precious. People are precious.

The loss of this gentleman this week reminded me I need to live today as though there is no tomorrow. I don't say that meaning I will go out and be irresponsible, which is what some may give themselves permission to do. What I mean by that is I need to love those around me today as though tomorrow is not promised. Somewhere along the line I believed into the idea that tomorrow will always be there to make up for what I didn't do today.

My days are numbered, yet I don't know what that number is. Neither do you.

I remember how discombobulated I was those first few days after I was diagnosed because I unknowingly convinced myself I had more control in my life than I really do. With the loss of this gentleman from our community this week, I am once again reminded of the lack of control we have in our lives. Yet I refuse to let fear be the outcome of this lack of control. I don't know the number of my days, but I know what I will choose to do with the days I have: I will choose to love others, deeply.

Love my family.

Love my friends.

Love my neighbors – the teachers, the mailmen, the bus drivers, the cashiers, the custodians, the elderly, the strangers – and seek ways to infuse love into our community… into the world.

I invite us all to take a moment to…

Pause. Breathe. Pray.

Take a moment to absorb that our days are numbered and how precious life is.

Take another moment to absorb that each person we pass each day is precious (maybe not to you in particular, but to someone).

I offer for you to join me and choose to use the time we have to live out love, moment by moment, day by day. I know from experience how transformative a practice this is, when it's practiced.

And although nothing makes sense as to why this gentleman lost his life, today let's choose to live out an act of love toward someone else in honor of his life, and his family.

LIFE LESSON
19
OUR DAYS ARE NUMBERED;
USE THEM WISELY

REFLECTION - APPLICATION

Take a moment to…
Pause. Breathe. Pray.

Reflection
♥ Notes to self about this life lesson:

_____

_____

_____

Application
♥ How will you apply this life lesson in your life?

_____

_____

_____

"Teach us to number our days, that we may gain a heart of wisdom."

— Psalm 90:12 (NIV)

LIFE LESSON

20

CELEBRATE THE LITTLE SUCCESSES

I went to my second post-op appointment yesterday and all is looking good. I've had my obturator adjusted twice and I'm sounding better every day. I can also officially drink from a cup! Yep, so long, syringe! Woo hoo! I will admit, drinking from a cup is not seamless. My children think it's comical that what goes in my mouth sometimes comes out my nose, but it's all part of the process.

Instead of dwelling on what is flawed, I am going to choose to celebrate the little successes along the way, like graduating to a cup!

Like anything else, this requires practice, and I will get better in time. I must admit, I do miss gulping down a glass of water; yet, rather than settling in there, I am choosing to draw myself back in to focus on what is going well, rather than what isn't.

Whatever your struggle may be, my hope for you is that you are also making forward strides, whether they are narrow or wide. I invite you to join me to...

Pause. Breathe. Pray.

And together let's celebrate the little successes along the way. Let's allow them to be fuel in our tank, giving us motivation to keep moving forward, moment by moment, day by day.

LIFE LESSON
20
CELEBRATE THE LITTLE SUCCESSES

REFLECTION ~ APPLICATION

Take a moment to…
Pause. Breathe. Pray.

Reflection
♥ Notes to self about this life lesson:

_____

_____

_____

Application
♥ How will you apply this life lesson in your life?

_____

_____

_____

"Rejoice always, pray continually."
— 1 Thessalonians 5:16-17 (NIV)

LIFE LESSON
21

WE NEED TO ASK FOR HELP

Giving oneself permission to rest is easier said than done.

I am just over two weeks post-op and I am doing well, overall. But now that I'm off meds and getting back into helping around the house (doing laundry, making lunches, bringing the kids to the bus stop and school, etc.) I realize life has not slowed down. It doesn't slow down for anyone.

I need to choose to slow down and rest, giving myself time to heal.

I am growing more aware there is a choice in front of me every day: I can get swept up into the tide of our day or I can choose to anchor myself and direct the use of my time throughout the day.

I need to direct the use of my time throughout the day.

As I mentioned, it is easier said than done. I have kind of thrown myself back into life, dismissing the reality that I am still healing. Yet today I'm granting myself permission to rest so I may heal. In order to do this though, I needed to ask for help from others. It wasn't easy to do this but I know I needed to.

I share this with you in case you have not given yourself permission to do the same. May you choose to ask for help so you may have space to rest and time to heal; for we all need healing in our own ways.

Maybe you also are healing from a physical injury or surgery.

Maybe you are going through a tumultuous moment in life with an illness or a relationship and need time to heal emotionally.

Maybe you are feeling anxious, depressed or are in the pit and you need to heal mentally.

Maybe you are disconnected, unplugged or are feeling spiritually off and you need time to heal spiritually.

I could go on and on.

The truth is, we all need time to rest. We need to give ourselves permission to slow down and heal. By doing so, we will come out on the other side more whole, more complete.

And so I offer that each of us take a moment to…

Pause. Breathe. Pray.

Let's ask ourselves: Where do I need healing? And then, let's choose to reach out and ask for help so we provide ourselves time and space to rest so we may move toward healing.

We can know this truth, or we can do it.

Rest and time to heal are necessities in life. I encourage you to come beside me today and let's humble ourselves to ask for help so we may truly heal.

LIFE LESSON
21
WE NEED TO ASK FOR HELP

REFLECTION ~ APPLICATION

Take a moment to…
Pause. Breathe. Pray.

Reflection
♥ Notes to self about this life lesson:

_____

_____

_____

Application
♥ How will you apply this life lesson in your life?

_____

_____

_____

"Come to me, all you who are weary and burdened,
and I will give you rest. Take my yoke upon you and learn from me,
for I am gentle and humble in heart, and you will find rest for your souls."
— Matthew 11:28-29 (NIV)

LIFE LESSON
22

SOMETIMES YOU HAVE TO DO
THE THINGS YOU DON'T WANT TO DO
TO GET THE RESULTS YOU NEED TO HAVE

Yesterday I spent the day at the doctor's office and then at urgent care. It turns out I was dehydrated, and a couple of other tests indicated why I had trouble getting out of bed yesterday.

I have had a killer sore throat for days and swallowing has been so painful, I've been limiting what I swallow, including waiting as long as possible before I *have to* swallow my own saliva.

As they determine how best to help me, I come back to this truth: Sometimes I have to do the things I don't want to do to get the results I need to have.

I don't want to eat or drink, but I need to.

I don't want to spend my days resting, but I need to.

I don't want to have my family and friends helping me take my kids to and from school, but I need to.

I don't want Stephen and my parents doing the laundry and other household chores right now, but I need to let them.

Surrendering to what *needs* to happen so I can heal is challenging but necessary.

I share this with you in case you needed to hear this truth, too.

I invite you to join me to take a moment to…

Pause. Breathe. Pray.

Let's surrender our desire of what we *want* to do to the truth of what *needs* to happen. This is true for so many areas of life:

- To deepen a relationship with a loved one requires saying no to time elsewhere and yes to time with them.
- Giving our children everything they want isn't what they need to grow into their best selves.
- If you are trying to get healthy or heal, it will take discipline to say yes to what nourishes you and no to what doesn't.

There are many more areas where this truth applies. Whatever struggle you are journeying through, please know I am walking a parallel one beside you. May we surrender to this truth and stop doing what we *want* to do and start doing the things we *need* to do, to get the results we need to have.

LIFE LESSON

22

SOMETIMES YOU HAVE TO DO THE THINGS YOU DON'T WANT TO DO TO GET THE RESULTS YOU NEED TO HAVE

REFLECTION ~ APPLICATION

Take a moment to…

Pause. Breathe. Pray.

Reflection
 ♥ Notes to self about this life lesson:

_____

_____

_____

Application
 ♥ How will you apply this life lesson in your life?

_____

_____

_____

*"Whoever wants to be my disciple must deny themselves
and take up their cross daily and follow me."*
— Luke 9:23 (NIV)

LIFE LESSON

23

RIDE THE WAVES WITH YOUR EYES FIXED ON GOD

The other night I saw a friend whose third child is due soon. I wished her well and shared with her a piece of advice my Aunt Barbara shared with me before labor that was helpful to me.

She told me to ride the waves of the contractions.

A contraction begins. It increases in intensity. It peaks. Then it decreases. And eventually the contraction ends. Then there is space (sometimes a tiny one) before the next contraction begins. Use that space to rest, gathering energy (physically, mentally, etc.) for the next contraction.

I loved this advice and carried it with me each time as I gave birth to our three children. As I was resting today, "riding the waves" popped into my head again – but not about labor. It was about riding the waves of life.

We all experience "contractions" in life. Whether it's tension in a relationship, parenting moments, the loss of a job, struggles in health, a move, etc. I am in the middle of a contraction with cancer. Over the past handful of days, I've had physical pain I started to believe was never going to end. Then I remembered this truth: This is temporary.

I need to…

Pause. Breathe. Pray.

And patiently persevere, riding the wave until this "contraction" passes – because it will pass.

I realize some of us are experiencing contractions that will take a few moments, while others are years into their contraction. I pray for all of us, that we may "run with perseverance the race marked out before us" (Hebrews 12:1) and ride the wave, fixing our eyes on Truth to get us through it.

No matter the cause of our contraction, may we remember its wave pattern – it starts, it rises, it peaks, it decreases, it ends. While we are in the contraction, let us…

Pause. Breathe. Pray

our way through it. And may we use our time between contractions to not stress, complain or fear the next one coming, but to enjoy the rest, and prepare our hearts, minds and Spirit for the next wave that will inevitably come.

LIFE LESSON
23
RIDE THE WAVES WITH YOUR EYES FIXED ON GOD

REFLECTION ~ APPLICATION

Take a moment to…
Pause. Breathe. Pray.

Reflection
♥ Notes to self about this life lesson:

_____

_____

_____

Application
♥ How will you apply this life lesson in your life?

_____

_____

_____

"I keep my eyes always on God.
With Him at my right hand, I will not be shaken."
– Psalm 16:8 (NIV)

LIFE LESSON

24

HE HOLDS YOUR HAND

When I heard the ENT say they thought it was cancer, he held my hand.

As the tears came flooding like a broken dam, he held my hand.

In the waiting room for every scan and test, he held my hand.

As we walked the path to and from the hospital, he held my hand.

Sitting on the couch, anxious as could be the night before surgery, he held my hand.

Driving to the hospital in the early morning as I played my calming music, he held my hand.

As I lay on the hospital bed, ready to go in for surgery, he held my hand.

When I woke up, a nurse went to get him so he could be beside me, holding my hand.

When I had an issue on day one post-op and I sat there crying in pain like I never had experienced before, he held my hand.

During the day he was there and at night he slept uncomfortably on chairs in case I needed his hand to hold.

We are waiting for the next step and, although I don't know what it will be like, I do know he will be there to hold my hand through it.

He is present. He is patient. He is kind. He is selfless. He is humble. He is never gives up, never loses faith, is always hopeful and endures through every circumstance.

He is love.

When I first wrote this I was writing about Stephen. He is my rock and has been a blessing for me, and for our children, through this journey.

When I went back and read what I wrote, I realized Stephen wasn't the only one holding my hand along the way, God has been holding my hand through this, too.

Often it is people we seek comfort in and I can't be more grateful that God uses Stephen every day as a vessel of His love (I am sure he will laugh, reading that!) but it's true. The way he loves me reflects the selfless love God has for each of us.

Yet people can't always be there. In surgery for example, Stephen wasn't there, but I knew God was with me, holding my hand.

God wants to be there beside us every step of the way, every day. I share this in case you too are going through a trial. Maybe you have someone to hold your hand, maybe you don't. Either way, I offer to you to always remember you are never alone.

May we take a moment to…

Pause. Breathe. Pray.

And trust God is there beside us. May we reach out. He is waiting to hold our hand through this, every step of the way.

LIFE LESSON
24
HE HOLDS YOUR HAND

REFLECTION ~ APPLICATION

Take a moment to…
Pause. Breathe. Pray.

Reflection
- ♥ Notes to self about this life lesson:

_____

_____

_____

Application
- ♥ How will you apply this life lesson in your life?

_____

_____

_____

"For I am your God who takes hold of your right hand
and says to you, Do not fear; I will help you."
— Isaiah 41:13 (NIV)

LIFE LESSON

25

WE MAKE OUR PLANS,
GOD DIRECTS OUR STEPS

I got the call today from my radiologist, who shared when I will start radiation and chemo. Radiation will be 35 rounds of treatment, five days a week for seven weeks, and chemo will be once a week during those seven weeks.

This wasn't part of my plan.

Cancer wasn't part of my plan.

Being apart from my family wasn't part of my plan.

Being a stay-at-home mom has provided me the opportunity to be a volunteer in my children's classrooms, at their schools, and see important milestones, like the last day of pre-K, and being able to go in to school for their birthday celebrations.

This year things will be different.

I will be getting the treatment I need, in a different state, Monday through Friday, until the end of their school year.

I will not sugarcoat this. It sucks.

Oh and my son's 10th birthday is in there, too. That's another punch in the stomach (although I'm determined to see him that day, somehow, some way).

I knew this was coming, but now the dates are real; and seeing what I will miss is clouding my vision. As I sit here,

Pausing. Breathing. Praying,

this verse popped into my head:

'We make our plans but God directs our steps.' – *Proverbs 16:9*

I never would have planned to have cancer, or to have to get treatments out of state. I never would have planned to have to miss part of my child's birthday, my little one's crossing-over-to-Kindergarten ceremony and other end-of-the-school-year milestones.

Yet, these are my God-directed steps.

I have to trust that behind this looming cloud, the radiant sun is shining. I have to believe this time away from my family is meant for good in the end. Not only to make me well physically, but to strengthen us individually, and as a family, and help us grow stronger in heart, mind and Spirit.

I know resisting what is to come will create more tension within me, and acceptance will give me freedom within.

I am choosing to resist today, simply because I need a day to sulk. I am feeling like a heartbroken mom who will miss her family. God knows my heart and He knows I'll move into acceptance soon... with His help.

We make our plans. God directs our steps.

I'll get there, God, accepting your plan. Today, just comfort me in my grief over what I hoped for that will not be...

... I wrote that yesterday and I meant every word. Yet so often a good night's sleep and widening the lens can bring perspective.

This morning I was able to take my eyes off my problem and widen my view to take in other happenings in the world. What I see is heartbreaking. There are so many people struggling in the world right now, and what I have to go through is nothing compared to some. There are those going through what I am going through without loved ones beside them. Some people's tumors are inoperable or treatment is unavailable to them. There is homelessness, addiction, San Bernardino, the Syrian chemical attack and South Sudan refugees and all their heartbroken families.

I know my struggle is real, but sometimes my gaze can be so narrow I forget to put it into perspective.

Today I am able to see my situation will be temporary. Today I am able to see blessings where yesterday I saw only obstacles.

I have the ability to get the care I need within reasonable driving distance of my home and family.

I have loved ones who will be in touch by phone and FaceTime to support me through the process and allow me to be present at activities I would otherwise have to miss.

I get to come home on weekends to watch my kids play softball, baseball and T-ball.

I have an amazing husband and three awesome kids I get to come home to.

Before I know it, my treatments will be over, and I will be back home, back to life as a stay-at-home mom with my kids home for summer break.

Maybe you're having a day like I did yesterday.

Be there.

Feel the grief of your situation.

It is real and it's okay for us to have days like that. When you are ready, I invite you to join me and...

Pause. Breathe. Pray.

Let's practice widening our lens. See the broader picture. Recognize often there are other situations that will give us perspective to what we are going through. When we are able to see the size of our struggle in the widened view, we can see our current situations may not be as bad as we first thought them to be.

We never would have devised this plan. But it is the path we are on and we need to walk these steps.

There is tension in resistance. There is freedom in acceptance.

I hope you will join me in trusting that God's plan is better than our own. Let us not look at the obstacles in our way but refocus our eyes to see the blessings He has put along the path. May we let go of our plans, and allow God to direct our steps.

LIFE LESSON
25
WE MAKE OUR PLANS,
GOD DIRECTS OUR STEPS

REFLECTION ~ APPLICATION

Take a moment to…
Pause. Breathe. Pray.

Reflection
 ♥ Notes to self about this life lesson:

_____

_____

_____

Application
 ♥ How will you apply this life lesson in your life?

_____

_____

_____

"We make our plans, but God determines our steps."
– Proverbs 16:9 (NLT)

LIFE LESSON
26

THE HARDER CHOICE
MAY BE THE WISER CHOICE

Having a rare cancer like I do – and with the tumor being in my palate and nasal cavity – my oncologist recommended proton-beam radiation coupled with low-dose chemo as part of my treatment plan, once I was healed from surgery.

Proton-beam radiation is different from regular radiation in that it's better targeted and, therefore, causes less collateral damage to surrounding cells.

Only 27 proton-beam radiation treatment centers exist in the United States; thankfully, one of them is in Boston, a couple of hours from my home in Connecticut.

My treatment would require me to have 35 rounds of proton-beam radiation and seven rounds of low-dose carboplatin-taxol chemotherapy.

When I first learned my treatment site was in Boston, Stephen asked if I wanted to drive to and from every day. My initial thought was yes. I wanted to be home with my family. But then I…

Paused. Breathed. Prayed.

And I realized staying in Boston was the wiser choice for me. As much as I love being with my family, I know three things that nourish me are my prayer time, being active and writing. If I were to be in the car upwards of six hours a day, it wouldn't give me the time, energy or space I needed to nourish myself.

I decided staying in Boston, away from my family, Monday through Friday for seven weeks was the better choice.

I felt strongly that I'd come back to them more whole at the end of each week, and at end of the treatment. I chose to use time away during those seven weeks to do what I needed to do to nourish myself and heal, rather than coming home daily, putting on a happy face and not really having time and space to process all I would be experiencing.

I share this with you in case you, too, need to have the wisdom to discern what is best. I invite you to join me to...

Pause. Breathe. Pray.

And may we have the courage to make the wiser choice, even if it is the harder choice.

LIFE LESSON
26
THE HARDER CHOICE
MAY BE THE WISER CHOICE

REFLECTION ~ APPLICATION

Take a moment to…
Pause. Breathe. Pray.

Reflection
♥ Notes to self about this life lesson:

_____

_____

_____

Application
♥ How will you apply this life lesson in your life?

_____

_____

_____

*"Making your ear attentive to wisdom
and inclining your heart to understanding"
– Proverbs 2:2 (ESV)*

LIFE LESSON
27

USE THE CALM TO
PREPARE FOR THE STORM

I'm in a strange place.

The surgery is over. My mouth is healing. I am eating food more and more, and my energy level is back to normal, for the most part. I have returned to the day-to-day tasks as a stay-at-home mom: making breakfast and lunches, getting kids off to school, doing the laundry, running errands, driving the kids to practices, etc.

Things are eerily normal.

This happened before.

After being diagnosed and going to a bajillion appointments, there were a couple weeks before my surgery when there was a calm. It was like nothing happened. Appointments stopped and I was suddenly back in my day-to-day routine as I had been prior to the day I was diagnosed. I knew the surgery was coming, but life didn't know that. It just went on, and I with it – going through my routine with the knowledge things would be different soon.

Then I had my surgery and things were different. I needed to heal, to rest, to figure out my new mouth. I had post-op appointments that slowly faded away and I am finding myself back in the calm.

There is a stillness and a silence here that is beautiful; yet in the same breath there is a quiet tension lingering, knowing on the horizon the next storm is waiting to arrive: radiation and chemo.

So this is where I am: in the calm before the next storm.

Some days I want to move things along. But then I reel myself in, knowing I need this time to heal – in body and mind – and stay grounded in Spirit. These calms, too, are a blessing for our children (and me) to have time to process each step slowly and get a break from the crazy, and settle back into a kind of normalcy.

These calms are an interesting place to be.

Do you also find yourself in that eerie place, the quiet calm before a known storm? If so, I invite you to join me to...

Pause. Breathe. Pray.

Although we may know the storm is coming, we don't know its potency. Let's take this time in the calm to be still with God, to practice trusting that the calm is there to give us space to prepare our hearts and minds for what is to come. Let's give thanks for the calm, and not look at this time as empty space, but use it to deepen our relationships with God and one another, so we are stronger to handle the storm headed our way.

LIFE LESSON
27
USE THE CALM TO
PREPARE FOR THE STORM

REFLECTION ~ APPLICATION

Take a moment to...
Pause. Breathe. Pray.

Reflection
♥ Notes to self about this life lesson:

_____

_____

_____

Application
♥ How will you apply this life lesson in your life?

_____

_____

_____

"Be still and know that I am God."
— Psalm 46:10 (NIV)

DIVINE APPOINTMENT

4

I've had a thyroid nodule for years. Back in 2009 I had a biopsy done; it was – thankfully – benign. Yet it is something I've needed to have tracked all these years.

One of my doctors wanted me to get an ultrasound on my thyroid to be certain all was well there. So off I went to another appointment, hopeful there were no changes to the nodule.

When I entered the office, the kind woman said hello and guided me back to the examination room. She asked what I did and out of nowhere, I responded, "I am an author."

Typically I say I am a stay-at-home-mom who writes, so I somewhat shocked myself that I stated it with such confidence. She asked what I wrote about, and I shared about my first book being about my struggles with anxiety and depression and my journey back to faith. Rather than tuning out, she leaned in closer, asking additional questions. Then, unexpectedly, she shared with me that she has struggled with anxiety and depression herself, and said she'd like to read what I wrote.

I had my backpack with me, filled with both of my books. I had started carrying them around with me in case I ran into someone I thought I could gift it too – so I offered her a copy of the book.

I don't know whether she read it or not but the fact that God continuously places people along my path to help me (or vice versa) has been such a blessing during this time. It helps me look beyond my struggle and observe how He is working in the midst of it.

KEEP YOUR EYES AND EARS OPEN
FOR **YOUR** NEXT DIVINE APPOINTMENT

LIFE LESSON

28

PATIENTLY PERSEVERE

Dealing with cancer is tough enough. Having insurance deny every doctor you see and your doctor's chosen treatment plan for you adds a layer of frustration no patient should have to deal with – but I have had to deal with this every step along the way.

Then, when I met with my radiologist the other day, she told me my insurance wouldn't cover the proton-beam radiation. They had appealed twice but said I should consider I might have to do regular radiation.

You'd think I would have been okay with that, considering the regular radiation facility is literally two miles from my home; but I was decidedly *not* okay with this.

All the doctors I saw, from New York, Connecticut and Boston, all said proton-beam would be best for my type of cancer and its specific location.

Oh, how I wish the people who were saying no could put themselves in my shoes and see which choice they would prefer if they were me.

I was not accepting "No" for an answer.

Thankfully, every time things were denied, after we called the insurance company, they were able to give me certain codes to help me get approved for the treatment every doctor believed was best for me.

What I am learning to do is to patiently persevere. It may take time, it may take energy, but by remaining patient and not throwing in the towel at the first – or even second – "No," thankfully, we got clearance to go ahead with the proton-beam radiation.

I share this side of my journey with you because we are going to meet obstacles along the way. Yes, one layer of a struggle is enough, but added layers just seem unnecessary and unfair. But they exist. And we can't change that.

I invite you to join me to...

Pause. Breathe. Pray.

And may we patiently persevere through every layer of our struggle, trusting they are part of the pruning process – growing us stronger in heart and mind as we stand firm in what we know is right.

LIFE LESSON
28
PATIENTLY PERSEVERE

REFLECTION ~ APPLICATION

Take a moment to…
Pause. Breathe. Pray.

Reflection
♥ Notes to self about this life lesson:

_____

_____

_____

Application
♥ How will you apply this life lesson in your life?

_____

_____

_____

"We rejoice in our sufferings,
knowing that suffering produces perseverance,
and perseverance produces character,
and character produces hope."
– Romans 5:3-4 (ESV)

115

LIFE LESSON
29

SOMETIMES WE NEED TO EXPERIENCE SHORT-TERM SUFFERING TO HAVE LONG-TERM FREEDOM

Seven weeks. That is a long time. Especially for our kids.

Stephen and I went through nine weeks of him in boot camp, two years of him in nuclear-power school and four years of him going in and out on the submarine, including two six-month deployments. I have no question we will get through this.

But the kids. It flat-out sucks to leave my kids. I know, between our loving family members, supportive friends and amazing community, they will be okay.

But it is hard.

I could surrender and choose another path of treatment and do the radiation here in town. Yet that could lead to more collateral damage and long-term side effects. The treatment all my doctors have recommended mean less collateral damage and fewer long-term side effects.

Ugh.

I know what is best. I need to experience the short-term suffering of being away from my family, so I have more freedom in the long term (so I pray).

I share this with you in case you also have a choice in front of you that is challenging you. I offer for you to join me to…

Pause. Breathe. Pray.

And let's be real with ourselves that sometimes we need to suffer in the short term for there to be long-term freedom. Yet it is tempting to do what will bring us freedom in the short term and not look ahead to the long-term suffering it may cause. Let's not give in to that temptation but do what is needed for there to be long-term freedom.

So, yes, I will be going to Boston for my treatments. I will choose for our family to endure this short-term suffering with the hope it will lead to my having a better quality of life during our many more years of life together.

LIFE LESSON
29
SOMETIMES WE NEED TO EXPERIENCE SHORT-TERM SUFFERING TO HAVE LONG-TERM FREEDOM

REFLECTION ~ APPLICATION

Take a moment to…
Pause. Breathe. Pray.

Reflection
♥ Notes to self about this life lesson:

_____

_____

_____

Application
♥ How will you apply this life lesson in your life?

_____

_____

_____

*"For our light and momentary troubles are achieving for us
an eternal glory that far outweighs them all."*
− 2 Corinthians 4:17 (NIV)

LIFE LESSON
30

THERE IS VALUE IN WAITING

I am waiting to go in to an appointment and there is an emergency on the floor. Lots of people are scrambling around to help the patient in need.

One of the many things I've learned through this time is that time spent waiting is not time wasted. Sitting and watching people go by gives me opportunities to pray for others. I don't know their stories, or what their outcomes will be, but I can wish the patient well and complete healing, I can pray their doctors have wisdom to know how to help, that the family is comforted and all will be well in time.

During my yoga training, we practiced a loving-kindness meditation instead of prayer, wishing those who crossed our path to be filled with lovingkindness, that they be well, peaceful, at ease, and that they be happy.

Whatever resonates with you, may we see the time we spend waiting – from grocery store lines, traffic jams, to waiting at an appointment – as opportunities to...

Pause. Breathe. Pray/Meditate for those around us.

We don't need to know their stories to wish them well. It makes the time go by and gives purpose to our thoughts (which could otherwise grow impatient and frustrated). So the next time you find yourself waiting, give it a try.

LIFE LESSON
30
THERE IS VALUE IN WAITING

REFLECTION ~ APPLICATION

Take a moment to…
Pause. Breathe. Pray.

Reflection
♥ Notes to self about this life lesson:

_____

_____

_____

Application
♥ How will you apply this life lesson in your life?

_____

_____

_____

"If we hope for what we do not yet have, we wait for it patiently."
— Romans 8:25 (NIV)

LIFE LESSON
31

INVITE GOD INTO THE EQUATION

The past few days, my head has been spinning. I've had people share with me stories of others who have cured their cancer with food, and stories of others who tried an all-natural approach but who passed away.

As my radiation and chemo treatments stand around the corner, doubt became a weed that began to grow in my mind. I had been confident with my choices, but when all these stories began flooding my way – and I enhanced their potency by using something called Google (I know, I know, "Lesson #2: Our Story Is Not Online" – it's an imperfect practice) and I started questioning the choices I had already prayerfully made.

As my mind began to spin, doubt seeped in and I began to question my path to healing. The yogi in me knows there is truth and healing power in foods, and the Christian in me knows God created this healing food and gifted people in the medical field with knowledge and wisdom to help others.

From day one I have been focused on healing, nutrient-dense foods; yet with the knowledge they didn't get clear margins in one area during my surgery (and there are cancer cells traveling along nerves), I know the Western treatments suggested can help, too.

The internal arguments grew intense.

Maybe, just maybe, I should *not* do the treatment and try healing with just foods.

No! You will look back and regret not doing the treatment if the cancer spreads.

True... but...

and around and around and around and around I spun.

When I realized I was listening to people rather than taking time to listen to God, I finally stopped talking about it (and Googling it) and took time to...

Pause. Breathe. Pray.

I took time to sit with God and asked, "What is the wisest choice for me?"

I sat.

No answer.

I sat some more.

No answer.

I sat some more and more... and more...

"Build a bridge."

Build a bridge? Okay. I will build a bridge.

I will integrate wisdom from both sides for my treatment and remain hopeful that I can raise awareness that there needs to be a bigger, wider bridge built between these two approaches.

You see, there is a disconnect between Western medicine and an integrative approach to healing. Some steps have been taken, but the huge gap I still see really saddens me. For example, from day one post surgery, I was offered a sugary protein drink and pudding. I declined and asked my sisters to go to Whole Foods and get me bone broth and unsweetened applesauce (not that I was able to eat either). Another example is when I was losing a bunch of weight post surgery, I was told to have milkshakes and ice cream – to get more calories in.

Nope.

When I know I have cancer still in me, why would I choose to put processed sugar – of any quantity but especially that amount – into my body and feed the cancer? (Yes, cancer feeds on sugar.) I want to starve these cells! Why not fuel up on foods that are known to fight cancer – such as turmeric with pepper, garlic, green leafy veggies, sprouts, green tea, celery, carrots (and SO much more!)?

In the same breath, these same doctors are able to send radiation up those nerves that are carrying the cancer and chemo increases the radiation's potency. So why wouldn't I try doing that too in the fight?

There is wisdom on both sides and I am building a bridge between them for my treatment plan. The wisest choice for me is to fuel my body, from the inside out, and also follow my radiation and chemo schedule. This may not be for everyone; but for me, being able to look my kids in the eyes and say, "I did all I could to fight this," brings me peace. I will look back with no what ifs, no regrets.

I am doing what is mine to do and trusting God with the rest.

If you, too, are spinning around, unsure what the wisest choice for you may be, I invite you to stop spinning (talking about it and Googling it) and take a moment to…

Pause. Breathe. Pray.

Invite God into the equation. And wait. Wait patiently. And trust where He leads you.

LIFE LESSON
31

INVITE GOD INTO THE EQUATION

REFLECTION ~ APPLICATION

Take a moment to…
Pause. Breathe. Pray.

Reflection
♥ Notes to self about this life lesson:

_____

_____

_____

Application
♥ How will you apply this life lesson in your life?

_____

_____

_____

"Come near to God and he will come near to you."
— James 4:8 (NIV)

DIVINE APPOINTMENT

5

After my first radiation treatment, Stephen and I decided to take a walk around Boston. We worked our way through Faneuil Hall on our way to the Freedom Trail.

As we walked along, we approached a musician playing guitar. As we got closer, I heard the song he was playing and it got me all choked up. Out of all the songs he could have been playing, he was playing our wedding song. I held Stephen's hand tighter as we stood there and enjoyed the little bit of the song that was left.

This was such a touching moment for me to be there, in Boston with Stephen on my first day of treatment and to have this musician playing our wedding song. This divine appointment gave my heart peace, as if God were saying to me, "You are where you need to be and I am right here with you two through this."

KEEP YOUR EYES AND EARS OPEN
FOR **YOUR** NEXT DIVINE APPOINTMENT

LIFE LESSON

32

LOVE IS THE BEST MEDICINE

My sister drove up from an hour away the day after I met with my ENT to be with us and help around the house while we were getting footing on what was happening. My parents were on a month-long road trip, and as soon as they heard, they turned the car around and came home. My other sister showed up that week too, and my brother flew in from California to see me as soon as he could. My in-laws came beside us in every possible way, too. Our aunts, uncles, cousins reached out our way. My sisters started a meal train, our friends donated towards a cleaning person; there was even a prayer gathering at church for our family.

Yes, I will be having chemo and radiation, and yes, I am sure I will need meds at time to help me with the pain. But the best medicine? The love being lived out toward us from the caring people in our lives.

I am not able to show up for others right now, but these people are showing up for our family. The love and light being poured toward the darkness our family is experiencing makes me speechless.

. . .

. . .

. . .

. . .

Okay, I guess I can't go speechless for too long here, but I truly can't express the full extent of the gratitude in my heart for the healing, the love people are sharing with our family through this time – from family, friends and our generous and thoughtful community...and beyond.

I share this with you because often we turn to *things* to help us heal. I wholeheartedly believe sometimes we need things but there is no thing we need more in life than the love of others.

And so I invite you to join me to...

Pause. Breathe. Pray.

No matter our struggle, may we all see the love and light flowing toward the darkness in our lives. And if we are in the darkness and see no light, may we take a step toward it ourselves. There are false lights, like over medicating, that can actually drag us deeper into darkness. May we step away from those and draw close to the people who live out love, because that is where we will find true love, which is the best medicine.

LIFE LESSON
32

LOVE IS THE BEST MEDICINE

REFLECTION ~ APPLICATION

Take a moment to…
Pause. Breathe. Pray.

Reflection
♥ Notes to self about this life lesson:

_____

_____

_____

Application
♥ How will you apply this life lesson in your life?

_____

_____

_____

"God is love."
— 1 John 4:8 (NIV)

LIFE LESSON

33

BE THANKFUL FOR
THE LITTLE THINGS

As I heal, I am realizing I have taken things like swallowing for granted. It's something we all do, yet when you are relearning how to use your mouth, like I am, it takes on a whole new perspective. I no longer am taking larger gulps when I am thirsty. Small sips are the best I can manage.

When you go to give your loved ones a kiss on the cheek and you realize you have to relearn how to kiss them because the way your mouth draws into a kissing configuration (think fishy face) doesn't work like it used to, you begin to see there are little things we do every day we give no thought to; yet, when they're taken away, you realize those little things are things to be thankful for.

I share this with you because I am seeing how the little things we do – like swallow and kiss someone on the cheek – are things I took for granted. It makes me wonder, if we were to be able to take a moment to...

Pause. Breathe. Pray.

And step back from the big picture problems and make a list of all the little things – from gulping down a glass of water to giving your loved ones a kiss on the cheek today – that we have to be thankful for, if it would then give new perspective to those big-picture problems. I believe joy doesn't come from the big things in life, but it comes from being able to give thanks for the little things in our lives each day that make up the big picture of our lives.

LIFE LESSON
33
BE THANKFUL FOR
THE LITTLE THINGS

REFLECTION ~ APPLICATION

Take a moment to…
Pause. Breathe. Pray.

Reflection
♥ Notes to self about this life lesson:

_____

_____

_____

Application
♥ How will you apply this life lesson in your life?

_____

_____

_____

"Every good and perfect gift is from above."
— James 1:17 (NIV)

LIFE LESSON

34

"I AM HEALING" IS A SUFFICIENT ANSWER

Family and friends mean well, but to be honest, when I get asked, "How are you?" I'm unsure how to respond these days.

Some days I'm well. Other days I'm not. Some days I'm able to walk to and from treatment without a thought in the world. Other days I need to pause and sit on the bench to rest. Some days I'm up and ready to take on the day, and some days, specifically Thursdays, are when I need to rest in bed all day, except when I go to my treatments.

Some days I'm home with my family and I feel well in my heart. I just want to go on a hike or bike ride with them, but the corner spot on the couch is where my body needs to rest as we watch a movie together instead.

When people ask me how I am, I don't want to give a fake answer; yet I don't need to disclose all that is on my heart.

My solution? I say, "I am healing."

That is the truth. I *am* healing, in different ways on different days.

I share this with you today in case you, too, have people asking you how you are and you are unsure of how to answer. I offer for you to…

Pause. Breathe. Pray.

And know that saying you are healing is a sufficient answer to give. We are all healing, in different ways, on different days. We don't need to pretend to be something we're not. We can honor the truth of our hearts with that simple, honest response.

LIFE LESSON
34
"I AM HEALING" IS A
SUFFICIENT ANSWER

REFLECTION ~ APPLICATION

Take a moment to…
Pause. Breathe. Pray.

Reflection
♥ Notes to self about this life lesson:

_____

_____

_____

Application
♥ How will you apply this life lesson in your life?

_____

_____

_____

"Speak the truth in love."
– Ephesians 4:15 (NIV)

DIVINE APPOINTMENT

6

On my first day of chemotherapy, I sat in the reclined chair, waiting for the Benadryl to kick in. My nurse first gave me Benadryl through my IV. It is given to help prevent a possible allergic reaction to the chemo drugs I would be receiving.

I watched my nurse get all geared up as she prepared the drip bags of taxol and carboplatin. As the Benadryl began to set in, I could tell I was feeling a little loopy. A lovely woman stopped by my door and asked if I wanted warm blankets. Before I had time to think, my mouth had already responded, "Yes." The 50 mg of Benadryl had shot through my veins and became like a truth serum.

As she walked in with the blankets, I asked her name and she said, "Esther."

I smiled and, once again, before I knew what my mouth was saying, I said I was reading the book of Esther.

Insert foot in mouth. Without these allergy-prevention meds in my system, there's no way I would've been so bold as to state that to someone I've just met.

She asked, "A book about a woman named Esther or the book in the Bible?"

I quickly blurted out, "The book in the Bible."

Okay, Benadryl, I see that with you I have no filter. Goodness gracious, how is this woman going to respond to my sharing that truth with her? I like to meet people where they are, not impose my stuff on them. Ugh!

Without blinking an eye, Esther walked toward me. She placed her hand on my arm and started praying over me.

This was not the response I was expecting, yet the words she spoke touched the deepest parts of my soul. She prayed beside me that day, telling me God has a purpose in this trial for me. She said sometimes we need to go through the valleys to get to the mountain top and God will use me in this for His will to be done and for His glory. Her life-affirming words encouraged me at the most critical part of my treatment, being infused with taxol and carboplatin, the chemo drugs.

The one prayer that captured my heart became the prayer I prayed while I lay there in my chemo chair every week: "Let the blood of Christ be infused through your veins."

I'll pause there because if someone had said that to me several years ago, I would have thought, *Well, that is just creepy.* Let me explain what it means to me now.

Jesus' dying on the cross is what we, as Christians, believe is the moment when Jesus took away all our impurities. He opened the door for us to be cleansed within. Therefore, His blood makes us clean. So when Esther chose to speak these words over me, rather than thinking the chemo was running through my veins, I pictured Jesus' blood washing through my veins instead, cleansing me from the toxins.

In this moment as my nurse hung the chemo bag to drip, I was incredibly calm and at peace because of this divine appointment with Esther.

Every Tuesday, as I sat in my chemo chair, I would repeat the prayer Esther gave me on that first day of chemo. I would pray over my veins for the washing away of the chemo drugs with the blood of Jesus, cleansing me from the inside out.

Although Esther had come in to my room to give me warm blankets to cover my body, it was her words of wisdom that covered and warmed my soul.

KEEP YOUR EYES AND EARS OPEN
FOR **YOUR** NEXT DIVINE APPOINTMENT

LIFE LESSON

35

CHOOSE TO BE GRATEFUL FOR THE BLESSINGS AROUND YOU

I read a story once about a professor who handed out a piece of paper to his class and asked them to write about what they saw. It was a sheet of white paper with a black dot on it. Once his students were done, he collected the papers. To his surprise, out of all of his students, only one wrote about the white space. Everyone else wrote about the black dot.

As I walked to chemo yesterday for the first time, I realized how chemo was a black dot in my day, and cancer is a black dot in my life. Yet, as I walked beside my mom to my appointment, we walked along a soothing river. The birds were chirping. We walked through green grass. There was so much beauty around us to soak in. I also received loving texts from family and friends throughout the day and had some incredible interactions with people I met here in Boston. I got to FaceTime my husband and kids last night and hear about their day. There was a lot of white space around my black dot.

But I know the opposite quite well. When I was in the pit with my anxiety and depression back in 2009, the dark was so blinding I could hardly see any light in my life. It can be so hard to focus on the smallest pinprick of light when the darkness is so consuming. Yet, as I renewed my mind and surrendered to receiving the help I needed, the white space grew and the darkness shrunk.

Those struggles were a stepping stone for me for this new battle I fight with cancer. I don't want my eyes to be so focused on my black dot, cancer, that I forget to see all the white space. Yet I know it doesn't just *happen*. I need to be intentional and directional with what I look at and listen to, because what goes into my mind matters. I am focused on feeding myself encouraging words every morning, meditating on truth and love, writing down all that I am grateful for, seeing outside myself and praying for others and their black dots. The white space isn't just available to me, it is available to you, as well.

In invite you to take a moment to…

Pause. Breathe. Pray.

Ask yourself, "How do I view my problems?" Are they little dots with a lot of good around them? Or are they all-consuming and leave you having trouble seeing any light?

If you are able to see the white space, the blessings around you, keep focusing on those; but if you are having trouble seeing the light, I encourage you to focus on one positive thing in your life today – it may be as simple as "I am breathing." I remember when I started this path, getting down to the basics of breath, food, shelter, clothing, shoes, etc. were my daily starting point.

We all need to start somewhere. Find your starting place and then, as you walk through your day today, purposefully seek out things to be grateful for. A flower blooming, your car starting, a green light, the sunshine, a child laughing, etc.

May we all take our focus off the black dot(s) in our lives and choose to see the white space, the blessings, around us today.

LIFE LESSON
35
CHOOSE TO BE GRATEFUL
FOR THE BLESSINGS AROUND YOU

REFLECTION - APPLICATION

Take a moment to…
Pause. Breathe. Pray.

Reflection
♥ Notes to self about this life lesson:

_____

_____

_____

Application
♥ How will you apply this life lesson in your life?

_____

_____

_____

*"Let us throw off everything that hinders and the sin that so easily entangles us.
And let us run with endurance the race that is set before us,
fixing our eyes on God."*
— Hebrews 12:1(NIV)

LIFE LESSON

36

CLOTHE YOURSELF IN LOVE

Every week I travel to Boston I pack the same clothes. It has made life easier to not think about what I am going to wear. I have never been the most fashionable person, but right now especially I really couldn't care less about how I look on the outside. I am focused on doing what I need to do to be more at peace within during my time in Boston while I, hopefully, get rid of this cancer.

A couple of dear friends and one of my sisters gifted me shirts with words on them such as "walk in love," "do not fear," "hope – faith – cure" and "family over everything." These are the shirts I wear to my treatments. I love putting them on and clothe myself in words that nourish my soul. I have always been a word person, loving song lyrics, poems, quotes, etc. Reading and listening to purposeful words helps bring calm and peace to my internal world. Now I wear them to wrap myself in what matters most: faith, love and people.

As much as I love walking with these soul-soothing messages on my shirts, I know they are just pieces of clothing. What I am learning in my quiet time with God is there are more important clothes for me to wear everyday.

What do I mean?

What we wear on the outside is not as significant as how we clothe our hearts and minds for the day. I know that may sound strange, but I spent the majority of life focused on how I looked on the outside. Now I start my days taking an inventory, not of my closet, but of my heart and mind. What I choose to put on in the morning matters and I have a choice along this walk with cancer of how I will dress my heart and mind. Yes, I could put on anger, bitterness, resentment, frustration, etc. But instead, each morning in my quiet time, I choose to clothe myself in compassion, kindness, humility, gentleness, patience, forgiveness and, above all, love, which binds all these together in perfect unity (Colossians 3:12-14). Yes, I literally sit in my prayer chair every morning, either at home or in the hotel, and picture myself getting dressed with these as my clothing. I can't change my circumstances, but I can choose what I wear every day.

I share this with you in case you, too, are in a struggle and find yourself wearing anger, bitterness, resentment, frustration, etc., today. I invite you to join me to…

Pause. Breathe. Pray.

Let's choose to take a moment to think about what we are wearing within our hearts and minds more than the clothing we put on our bodies today. May we also take a moment to ask ourselves what we want people to see when they look our way? Compassion or judgment? Kindness or bitterness? Gentleness or anger? Patience or impatience? Forgiveness or resentment? Love or hate?

May we choose to put on compassion, kindness, gentleness, patience, forgiveness and, above them all, may we clothe ourselves with love. Out of all the clothes we can wear, love is the most beautiful garment of all.

LIFE LESSON
36
CLOTHE YOURSELF IN LOVE

REFLECTION ~ APPLICATION

Take a moment to…
Pause. Breathe. Pray.

Reflection
♥ Notes to self about this life lesson:

_____

_____

_____

Application
♥ How will you apply this life lesson in your life?

_____

_____

_____

"Clothe yourselves with compassion, kindness, humility, gentleness and patience… forgive one another if any of you has a grievance against someone. Forgive as God forgave you. And over all these virtues put on love, which binds them all together in perfect unity."
— Colossians 3:12-14 (NIV)

LIFE LESSON
37

BEING WELL BEGINS WITHIN

I have lost about 20 pounds from my surgery and treatments. Truthfully, it is a weight I used to be and would ideally love to remain at it (maybe it's wrong to admit but I'm just being real with you). Yet when I think about what got me to this weight, I would prefer to have the extra 20 pounds and not have had cancer.

Having lost the weight, old thoughts come back, thoughts I'd dealt with in the past regarding body-image issues. I think about how the weight will come back on in time. I don't know how much or how soon, but I have to remember being a certain weight or size is insignificant to being at peace within.

I spent so much of my life thinking if I looked good on the outside, then I would finally be at peace on the inside. What I came to learn was peace within comes from being still and knowing God. Nothing, no thing, I did to make myself look better on the outside gave me the peace I have received from starting to live from the inside out, with love as my core.

I share this with you because maybe you, too, are thinking if you look better on the outside, your inside will finally be at peace.

I can say to you from my walks with anxiety, depression and now cancer, I am at peace within, not because I am a certain weight, but because every day I wake up and focus on fueling my heart, mind and Spirit for the day.

I invite you to join me to…

Pause. Breathe. Pray.

And may we always remember, no matter what size we are, being well within is more important than being a certain weight or size. May we each take time to fuel our heart, mind and Spirit today.

LIFE LESSON
37
BEING WELL BEGINS WITHIN

REFLECTION ~ APPLICATION

Take a moment to…
Pause. Breathe. Pray.

Reflection
- ♥ Notes to self about this life lesson:

_____

_____

_____

Application
- ♥ How will you apply this life lesson in your life?

_____

_____

_____

"My soul finds rest in God alone…my hope comes from Him."
— Psalm 62:1 & 5(NIV)

DIVINE APPOINTMENT

7

Every day I carry a backpack. In it I always have at least one of each of my books, *My Journey to Live From the Inside Out* and *A Place for Sam*. I always wanted to have them if there was someone I met to whom I could pass one along to as an act of love.

One day I was walking with my Mom back from Whole Foods, which is around the corner from Mass General. There was a father and son walking together beside us. The son was about three. As we waited at the corner of the street for the light to tell us to walk, the boy and I exchanged smiles. My mind immediately thought, "Give him a *Sam* book." After crossing the street, I asked the father if he was okay with my passing the book along to his son. He was fine with it, and with the book I also gave the boy one of the glow-in-the-dark wristbands that says, "You are unique, valuable and loved."

After I gave it to them they continued on, but I heard, "Excuse me, Miss. Excuse me. Can I have one of those too?"

When I looked up, there was a woman waving me her way. I approached her and asked if she wanted a book or a bracelet. She asked for the bracelet and then asked for an extra one for her friend beside her. I said yes and started rummaging in my backpack for the bracelets when she said, "You're a Christian, aren't you?"

Surprised by her unexpected question, I told her I was. What she said next will always stay with me. She shared that she and her friend were down on their luck and asked if I would pray with them.

This wasn't something I was accustomed to doing, but I knew God put me in this spot for this moment. And on the side of the street in Boston, with Mom beside me, we gathered in a small circle with this lovely couple and prayed with them.

What struck me the most afterward was that, out of all the things this homeless couple could have asked for, they asked for prayer, which was something I could give them in that moment.

Their names are forever in my heart and my prayer journal, and I thank God for giving me a divine appointment like this one, in the midst of my struggles, to remind me just because I'm experiencing what I am doesn't mean I can't come beside someone else and be a blessing to them.

KEEP YOUR EYES AND EARS OPEN
FOR **YOUR** NEXT DIVINE APPOINTMENT

LIFE LESSON
38

SCATTER SEEDS OF LOVE

At the end of last week, I wasn't feeling great. Not sure if it was the treatments, being homesick or a combination of both. I was ready to go home by Friday and be with my family, back in our home, in my hometown.

On arriving home, I was greeted by a Box of Sunshine from a local Girl Scout troop. It was filled with encouraging notes and yummy treats for our family. It definitely filled my heart, and then as I watched my children's grinning faces as they read the personalized messages, my heart burst with joy and gratitude.

This Box of Sunshine was a seed of love scattered our way that made our world more beautiful.

The night before I left for Boston last week, I read one of my favorite books to my children, *Miss Rumphius*. If you're unfamiliar with the story, it is about a well-traveled lady, Miss Alice Rumphius, whose goal in life is to make the world a more beautiful place. She realizes she can do so by scattering lupine seeds around her town, every year bringing beauty to her quaint coastal town.

After reading the book with my children, I reminded them of the Sunshine box they received and how people were scattering seeds of love our way and to receive that love with an open heart. I encouraged them last week to notice seeds of love that are being scattered their way and to scatter their unique seeds this week along their path. All these seeds of love being scattered, whether the receiver or the giver, make the world more beautiful.

Last night I asked them if they had any stories to share from their day about any seeds of love they scattered or any that came their way… and they had all forgotten about it. (This is reality, my friends, not a perfect picture I am painting for you.)

The truth is, whether or not they choose to do as I have encouraged them, the lesson from *Miss Rumphius* – making it a goal in life to make the world more beautiful place by using our unique gifts – is planted in their hearts. My hope is they are able to see the seeds of love scattered our way during this time, like the Box of Sunshine. And when it's on their hearts to scatter their seeds of love, they will – and the world will be a more beautiful place because of it.

It is on my heart this week to see the seeds being scattered our way *and* to scatter seeds along my path. I invite you to…

Pause. Breathe. Pray.

And join me today, keeping your eyes and ears open for where love is needed and choose to scatter seeds of love in that direction today, using your unique seeds, and remember to also give thanks for love you gather from the seeds that are tossed your way.

LIFE LESSON

38

SCATTER SEEDS OF LOVE

REFLECTION ~ APPLICATION

Take a moment to…
Pause. Breathe. Pray.

Reflection
♥ Notes to self about this life lesson:

_____

_____

_____

Application
♥ How will you apply this life lesson in your life?

_____

_____

_____

"Whoever sows generously will also reap generously."
— 2 Corinthians 9:6 (NIV)

LIFE LESSON
39

YOU ARE NEVER ALONE

Our daughter heard about the Relay for Life event at school a number of weeks ago and was determined to create a team and raise money and awareness for cancer research.

Yesterday was the event. At one point in the day, I sat in a chair for survivors (which was surreal) next to other survivors. Then someone asked whether I had looked behind us yet. I said no, then turned around and saw this crowd of people, of all ages.

It brought me to tears.

Although we may lie alone in the MRI and CT scan machines, or on the radiation tables, and sit in our chemo chairs solo, please remember we are never alone.

When I saw this view yesterday, it showed me that, beyond our family and friends, there are communities and organizations at work through events like Relay for Life who are working to raise awareness and funds to find a cure for all our cancers – and for what you are struggling with too.

Tomorrow when I am back on that table getting radiation, I will be carrying this view in my heart.

Thank you to every family member, friend and stranger fighting this battle with us. You are a gift and strengthen my heart in this battle.

When my 11-year-old stood up as they honored caregivers yesterday, I wept.

My sweet child has had her three closest girls – my mom, our dog and me – all get cancer in the past two years. That is not cool, cancer. But you are messing with the wrong family *and* the wrong girl. Because this 11-year-old won't let cancer crush her Spirit. Instead, she chose to stand up and rally her family and friends to raise money and awareness to find a cure for this disease.

She is strong, she is determined, she has a heart full of love; and with her in this battle, cancer should be afraid… very afraid.

I share this with you because no matter your struggle, there is a crowd of people, those determined daughters and sons, who are fighting to make the struggle go away.

If you are feeling alone, please take a moment with me to…

Pause. Breathe. Pray.

And if you are feeling alone, reach out. Know you are not alone. There are those people wanting and waiting to help you. Please reach out and let them come beside you to support you.

As humbling as it may be, we need their support right now.

*On a side note, when I was revising this chapter, I asked my daughter what life lesson she learned from this experience and she said, "NEVER GIVE UP!"

I thought that was another life lesson learned through this walk that was worth sharing with you.

LIFE LESSON
39

YOU ARE NEVER ALONE

REFLECTION ~ APPLICATION

Take a moment to…
Pause. Breathe. Pray.

<u>Reflection</u>
♥ Notes to self about this life lesson:

_____

_____

_____

<u>Application</u>
♥ How will you apply this life lesson in your life?

_____

_____

_____

"Encourage one another and build each other up."
— 1 Thessalonians 5:11 (NIV)

LIFE LESSON
40

IN GIVING, WE RECEIVE

One of my soul sisters has given me an envelope for every day I am away for my treatments. She drops them off on Sundays so I can have them for the week ahead. These envelopes are filled with drawings from her kids, encouraging notes/verses, and a joke a day. It is a gift every day to open up each envelope and see the love flowing out at me. She knows me well and knows I love giving to others. One thing she has done is each week she's given me a gift card to give away.

How awesome is that?! I just love it!

When I walk through the streets, I am keeping my eyes up, looking for who could use the blessing. When I pass the gift cards along, it fills me with such joy! I am so grateful for my dear friend, for her thoughtfulness and for her giving me sight to see beyond myself and my struggles and to keep my eyes and heart open to bless those around me who need someone to live out love their way.

I invite you too to take a moment and…

Pause. Breathe. Pray.

Are you also wrapped up in your struggle today? If so, I get it, but let me encourage you to take a moment today to look beyond your struggle and see if you can be a blessing to someone else in some way today. From a loved one, to a stranger, do one thing with love as its foundation and see how your heart feels afterward. It may not take away our struggles, but it will help renew our Spirit, even if for a moment.

LIFE LESSON
40
IN GIVING, WE RECEIVE

REFLECTION ~ APPLICATION

Take a moment to…
Pause. Breathe. Pray.

Reflection
♥ Notes to self about this life lesson:

_____

_____

_____

Application
♥ How will you apply this life lesson in your life?

_____

_____

_____

"Let each of you look not only to his own interests,
but also to the interests of others."
– Philippians 2:4 (ESV)

LIFE LESSON

41

THERE'S A LAST TIME
FOR EVERYTHING

I just had a moment I've captured deep in my heart.

I got home today from being gone for the week in Boston getting my radiation and chemo treatments. We had a nice family night and did our normal bedtime routine with the kids. Stephen and I had come downstairs and I assumed my corner spot on the couch, ready to cozy up with my blanket and favorite guy when I heard the pitter patter of feet above me.

My little guy was up.

I heard him round the corner, run down the stairs, and then he found his way beside me on the couch. When I asked what he needed, he said he just wanted to snuggle.

And snuggle we did. Then something happened that hasn't happened in forever, my little guy fell asleep on me. I can't remember the last time he did that, and I don't know whether he'll ever do it again, because he's almost five.

I sat there, as still as possible, taking in his sweetness and cherishing this moment.

Brad Paisley has a new song, "Last Time for Everything," and we've listened to it a lot recently. In that moment as I held my youngest in my arms, I couldn't help thinking this might be the last time he (or any of my children) falls asleep on me. It also made me pause to think about how many "last times" I've experienced in life that I never realized were my last times. I was thankful I recognized this as one, and I treasured every moment of it.

I know our lives can be busy, and we may be rushing around or stuck in our struggles, but I invite you to join me to…

Pause. Breathe. Pray.

Cancer or not, may we all embrace how precious time is and cherish the beautiful moments we get, the expected and the unexpected, because there *is* a last time for everything.

LIFE LESSON
41
THERE'S A LAST TIME
FOR EVERYTHING

REFLECTION ~ APPLICATION

Take a moment to…
Pause. Breathe. Pray.

Reflection
♥ Notes to self about this life lesson:

_____

_____

_____

Application
♥ How will you apply this life lesson in your life?

_____

_____

_____

"Be very careful, then, how you live—not as unwise but as wise,
making the most of every opportunity."
— Ephesians 5:15-16 (NIV)

LIFE LESSON

42

SOMETIMES YOU JUST NEED TO LAUGH

For Mother's Day, I was welcomed into my morning with a lovely breakfast Stephen made. My daughter turned our Lego-filled dining-room table into a delightful place for us to gather for breakfast and our boys served up my meal.

I grew emotional as we sat there together, eating, talking and laughing. I got choked up a few times, having an honest moment in my head that I needed to treasure this moment, hoping it wouldn't be my last Mother's Day with them.

I unwrapped their thoughtful gifts, like a sun hat to help me shield my radiation-burned face from the sun. I was overwhelmed in the moment, so grateful to be here with my family and hopeful there would be many more Mother's Day celebrations ahead, with us gathering around the table together, sharing meals and stories, laughing and crying together.

I decided that morning we needed to go and have some fun together. I had the energy and so I suggested we go bowling.

When we finished up bowling, our boys were asking to play laser tag. The pre-cancer me would have been hesitant, but in this moment I simply thought, *Another fun memory made with my family... Why not?!*

We went in to play laser tag and found we were the only players there. We had the entire place to ourselves! We got the gear on, listened to the directions and headed into the dark room lighted by neon-colored black lights. I had not laughed that hard in a long time. We had the time of our lives!

I share this with you in case you tend to be on the more serious side of life (like me) and think more than you laugh. I invite you to join me to…

Pause. Breathe. Pray.

And let's give ourselves the gift of laughter. Whether it's a movie we watch solo or we get together with loved ones and do something like play laser tag, may we remember sometimes we just need to simply laugh and have some good ol' fun to nourish our soul.

LIFE LESSON
42
SOMETIMES YOU JUST NEED TO LAUGH

REFLECTION ~ APPLICATION

Take a moment to...
Pause. Breathe. Pray.

Reflection
♥ Notes to self about this life lesson:

_____

_____

_____

Application
♥ How will you apply this life lesson in your life?

_____

_____

_____

"Enjoy what you have rather than desiring what you don't have."
— Ecclesiastes 6:9 (NLT)

LIFE LESSON

43

TRUST IN GOD'S TIMING

While I was home over the weekend, one day I was in the shower. I was washing my hair and when I washed out the shampoo, a bunch of hair came out onto my hand. As I raked my hand through my hair, more hair came out. Again and again this happened.

What?! This is not supposed to be part of the process. I am having low-dose chemo, I shouldn't be losing my hair.

I collected the hair that came out and after the shower I showed Stephen. He assured me it was fine and said to mention it to my oncologist on Tuesday, my chemo day.

At my appointment with my oncologist that week, I shared that my hair was falling out. Not everywhere but it was definitely thinning in the back, in the center of my head. He assured me it was part of the process. He shared that I was on taxol, which at a high dose has 100% hair loss, but with low dose, the hair will only thin. He also stated that sometimes hair loss occurs from radiation, as well.

Why didn't they tell me this before? Why did I have to find out by losing my hair? Maybe people find out from researching their treatments, but I am someone who asks Stephen to read the side effects because if I read them, I'd probably create them in my mind! I have a good relationship with my doctors, and I was surprised they didn't advise me to expect this. He said it was part of the process but my hair would thin and not to expect to lose it all.

Receiving this information was hard. Another unknown thrown into the equation. My hair will thin. By how much?! Do I need to cut it? Shave it? I'm not sure.

I called a dear friend who has had her own walk with cancer and shared this situation. Her response was beautiful. She said she learned if doctors told her everything up front, she would probably have lost her mind. But getting the information over time gives us the ability to digest it in small quantities, rather than all at once.

She was right. I didn't need to know this until now. What good would it have done me to know ahead of time except to possibly have me worrying more about when it would happen? My heart settled into the truth that this was happening in God's timing.

What do I mean by that?

Yes, it would have been nice to be told about this earlier, but was it necessary? I could be upset I wasn't told sooner but I believe God's timing is perfect. Although often the timing of things doesn't make sense to us, I have to trust that His timing is better than mine. Rather than belaboring over wishing things were different, by trusting that God's timing is perfect, I've shifted into a more peaceful place, even with this unknown lingering of how much hair I will lose.

I share this with you in case you, too, feel like the timing of things in your life is not what it should be. I invite you to join me to...

Pause. Breathe. Pray.

Although we see all pieces in our life puzzle scattered around without the cover of the box to help us put the picture together, God is the puzzle maker and sees how all these scattered pieces come together to form the beautiful story of our lives. And with that visual in mind, may we let go of what we think is the best timing for things and trust that God's timing is exactly what it needs to be.

LIFE LESSON
43
TRUST IN GOD'S TIMING

REFLECTION ~ APPLICATION

Take a moment to…
Pause. Breathe. Pray.

Reflection
♥ Notes to self about this life lesson:

_____

_____

_____

Application
♥ How will you apply this life lesson in your life?

_____

_____

_____

"God has made everything beautiful in its time."
— Ecclesiastes 3:11(ESV)

LIFE LESSON

44

IT'S IN THE BROKEN PLACES
LIGHT CAN SHINE THROUGH

As I lay on the radiation table a couple of weeks ago, I realized I was gripping the handles I usually hold on to. I was thinking about the radiation and wrapping my thoughts around it working, hitting the right places, getting deep enough in my nerves, etc. And then it hit me: My body is broken.

With or without cancer, my body will age. It will weaken. It will eventually fail. That is the truth. I don't say this with sadness or seeking pity. I say it with confidence because this view of my body heals my soul.

What do I mean?

My body is something I have taken care of most of my life – but for vain purposes. Years ago, as I shared in my book, *My Journey to Live From the Inside Out*, I realized I was living from the outside in, trying to take care of the outside of myself so I would feel whole within. What I came to learn is that taking care of the inside -- my heart, mind and Spirit -- first helped me grow content with who I am on the outside.

As I've journeyed to live from the inside out, nourishing my Spirit within before my physical appearance, I've received so much peace within. Yet, as I say in the title of the book, it is a journey, and at times I find myself living once again from the outside in – in this case, seeking to cling to my body.

When I noticed my hands were clenched on the handles, I released my grip and opened my palms to God. I had an honest conversation, telling God my desires: to be here, to live a full life with my family, to grow old with Stephen and watch the kids grow into adults, etc. And then I surrendered my body to God – again.

I don't mean I am giving up, but this battle isn't in my hands, really. In that moment I gave my body to God, trusting Him with the outcome of this whole cancer thing.

Instead, I asked God how I can be used, in this broken body, to live out love while I am blessed to be here to do so.

And as I lay there on the table, I was drawn to pray for others – my family, friends, people whose paths I have crossed in my time here in Boston. Being able to spend the time on the table loving on others rather than gripping those handles and trying to make my body not be broken is healing in its own way. I may be broken in body, but I'm whole in Spirit.

I know it isn't an easy journey to be here – and I'm sure I'll circle away from and back to this truth many more times – but I wholeheartedly believe this is the way we are meant to live, from the inside out – nourishing our Spirit first and trusting the rest will follow.

It's a truth many of us don't want to admit. I happen to have met this truth eye to eye with cancer that our bodies are temporary, but our Spirit is eternal.

I invite you to join me to take a moment to…

Pause. Breathe. Pray.

And if you have been struggling with trying to remain whole, I want to give you permission to admit you are broken. Maybe you are broken in body, maybe in mind, maybe in Spirit. However, you are broken, trust that part of the healing process is to finally let go of trying to be whole and simply say, "I am broken."

Trying to be whole is the way of the world. The way of peace is to acknowledge it is a blessing to be broken — for it is in the broken places light can shine through.

My hope for each of us is to let go of having to be whole and perfect. Instead, may we embrace our brokenness. May we allow the light of love to shine through those broken spaces, healing us from the inside out, so we may live a fuller life as the people we were made to be.

LIFE LESSON
44
IT'S IN THE BROKEN PLACES
LIGHT CAN SHINE THROUGH

REFLECTION ~ APPLICATION

Take a moment to…
Pause. Breathe. Pray.

Reflection
♥ Notes to self about this life lesson:

_____

_____

_____

Application
♥ How will you apply this life lesson in your life?

_____

_____

_____

"What I tell you in the dark, speak in the light;
what is whispered in your ear, proclaim from the roofs."
— Matthew 10:27 (NIV)

DIVINE APPOINTMENT

8

When I arrive at radiation, the thoughtful radiation team always asks if I would like to listen to music during my treatment. Often I choose silence, but this particular day I did ask for music. I specified a station that plays songs that nourish my soul.

As I settled onto my back, with the white hospital blanket covering my body, one of the well-trained team members came over to snap my radiation face mask onto the table, to be sure I was secure and wouldn't move my head during treatment.

As I lay there with my obturator out and a device like a baby's pacifier in my mouth, to hold my tongue down, I reached my hands down to find the handles, to be sure my shoulders were lowered. I relaxed my hands and opened them up toward God.

Often while I lie there, I picture Jesus kneeling beside me, holding my right hand. That image brings me peace. As I rested there on the table, a song came on and my heart smiled as a tear or two rolled down my cheek.

The song that played is called "Broken Things" by Matthew West. The lyric read,

> *"The pages of history they tell me it's true*
> *That it's never the perfect;*
> *It's always the ones with the scars that You use*
> *It's the rebels and the prodigals; it's the humble and the weak*
> *All the misfit heroes You chose*
> *Tell me there's hope for sinners like me…*
> *…But if it's true You use broken things*
> *Then here I am Lord, I'm all Yours"*

The divine appointment warmed my heart. I had just written Life Lesson #44: It's in the Broken Places Light Can Shine Through *that* morning. To lie on the radiation table after writing that, and to hear this song for the first time, confirmed for me God was with me and telling me yes, my body may be broken, but He will use broken things.

My response?

"Here I am, Lord. I'm all yours."

KEEP YOUR EYES AND EARS OPEN
FOR **YOUR** NEXT DIVINE APPOINTMENT

LIFE LESSON
45

SOLITUDE RENEWS THE SPIRIT

I just got home after another week in Boston. I'm in my home alone and I love it! I know this may sound odd. Of course I love being with my family, but to have a little bit of solitude before reuniting with my family is a gift – for me, and for them. In solitude I enjoy the stillness and silence, for this is when the chaos calms, my mind clears and I recharge my batteries.

Don't get me wrong. I love being with people. Yet for the past five weeks, someone has been with me 24/7. From car rides to doctors appointments, grocery outings, you name it, I am with someone. I'm extremely grateful for each person who has taken a week of their time to be with me in Boston; my husband, mom, dad, aunt, sister and friends. Without them I would probably not eat, and they help me take care of the little things that are so helpful, like getting me my water and tea, when I am low on energy, which seems to be more and more these days. Yet I am always with someone. I'm not waking up bright and early like I used to, so even my morning time is usually with other people present these days. It is what is needs to be but...

I need time alone. Solitude renews my Spirit. It is different from being lonely. Loneliness* is when you're alone, feeling isolated and low. Solitude is when you're content in aloneness and, in that time, you are renewed. Solitude is my respite from the craziness of the world and my situation.

I am going to soak up every moment of solitude I get right now to fuel up for my time with my family this afternoon. If you, too, are needing to recharge, I invite you to take a moment to...

Pause. Breathe. Pray.

And rest for a moment, or two, in solitude.

Sometimes, for me, it means not making that phone call, or turning off the radio and just driving in silence. Sometimes I pull up my driveway, turn off the car and sit alone before heading in to the house. Sometimes it's sitting on my chair on our patio, looking at our yard, simply enjoying the quiet. Whatever it looks like for you, take the time to enjoy your solitude. May our time alone renew our Spirit for what lies ahead.

*And if you are feeling lonely, isolated and low, please don't stay alone; reach out to someone who will come beside you. If you're in the U.S. or Canada, you can always call 2-1-1, the National Suicide-Prevention hotline – 1-800-273-8255, or 9-1-1 in an emergency situation – for help.

LIFE LESSON
45
SOLITUDE RENEWS THE SPIRIT

REFLECTION ~ APPLICATION

Take a moment to...
Pause. Breathe. Pray.

Reflection
♥ Notes to self about this life lesson:

_____

_____

_____

Application
♥ How will you apply this life lesson in your life?

_____

_____

_____

*"Create in me a pure heart, God,
and renew a steadfast spirit within me."*
— Psalm 51:10 (NIV)

LIFE LESSON

46

THE STRUGGLE IS REAL,
BUT THERE IS HELP

Mouth sores. Trouble swallowing. Constant pain.

Why is it so hard for me to take meds?!

I have been up since three something. My mouth is in pain. I have made it so far through my treatments on lidocaine, magic mouthwash, aloe juice and Tylenol. But the past 24 hours, those aren't cutting it. I know meds are a blessing, but I really struggle with choosing to go on them.

I've been here before.

Last time was in 2010. I was battling my deepest pit of anxiety and depression. I remember being in the kitchen, crying to Stephen because I felt like a failure having to get to the point where I needed meds to help me. What I learned from that experience is meds can be a blessing; they were a stepping stone for me to reach the solid ground I'm on today.

Yet, for almost two hours, this little pill has had my mind running in circles again... deciding whether to take it.

I'm hopeful it will help, yet I already have so much being put into my body on a weekly basis with chemo. Last week I actually watched as the nurse donned her special gloves and gown in order to give me my chemo. She was all geared up to ensure none of the chemo meds touched her; but I was about to get them infused right into my bloodstream. Pretty crazy, right?

Anyway, I'm waving the white flag. It hurts even to swallow my own saliva at this point and I need to rest. I know I need to surrender and trust that these meds are a blessing. I just wish the old me would remind the new me it's okay and I'm no less of a person because I got to this point. I would never judge another person who chose to take meds, so why should I judge myself?

Anyway, if you're like me and struggle with taking meds, I hope you'll join me and...

Pause. Breathe. Pray.

May we have the wisdom to know what is the wisest choice, and the courage to make that choice – even when it's the hard thing to do. The struggle is real, but there *is* help for us, and sometimes that help comes in a little pill.

(sip of water... gulp)

LIFE LESSON
46
THE STRUGGLE IS REAL,
BUT THERE IS HELP

REFLECTION ~ APPLICATION

Take a moment to…
Pause. Breathe. Pray.

Reflection
♥ Notes to self about this life lesson:

_____

_____

_____

Application
♥ How will you apply this life lesson in your life?

_____

_____

_____

"Do not be afraid, for I am with you, do not be discouraged,
for I am your God, I will strengthen you and help you."
— Isaiah 41:10 (NLT)

LIFE LESSON
47

SERVE PEOPLE, NOT MONEY

I've hit another bump in the road with insurance. I say "another" because we've hit bumps at every step along the way so far. Thankfully it's always worked out, so I'm hopeful this time will yield the same outcome.

I share this because I get disheartened when I think about how companies make decisions at times about what is best for them *financially*, rather than what is best for the person they are supposed to be serving, especially when it comes to their health and well being. Seeing people serve money over people is backwards from how we are called to live.

We are to serve people over money.

So often, money can blind us from seeing how things really are and what really needs to happen. I know this because money has blinded me many times from putting people first. Can you relate to any of these situations?

Have you ever had an argument over money with a loved one? Isn't your relationship more important than money?

How often do we pass over opportunities to help others in need (even a small donation of a dollar or two)? Isn't helping a person in need more significant than the thing we'd spend that dollar or two on? And isn't it interesting when we have a need, or even a want, the money is available?

I used to live serving money. It drove me, it drove my decisions, and still (at times) blurs my vision. Yet I have experienced the freedom of putting people first and trusting my needs will be met when I put people over money.

So when I was told at first the obturator, that will help me speak articulately and eat, would not be covered, I was reminded how, rather than looking at a person and their unique situation, they are evaluating numbers to make their choice.

I pray they see me instead of numbers.

And if you can relate to that struggle, I hope they see *you* instead of numbers, too.

I invite us all to take a moment to…

Pause. Breathe. Pray.

And if we find ourselves being tempted to serve money over people, may we choose to put people first. When we put into practice placing people over money, it will make a difference in our hearts, and in the hearts of those we are helping. By making others a priority, we're letting them know we acknowledge their needs and would like to be a part of the solution.

LIFE LESSON
47

SERVE PEOPLE, NOT MONEY

REFLECTION ~ APPLICATION

Take a moment to…
Pause. Breathe. Pray.

Reflection
♥ Notes to self about this life lesson:

_____

_____

_____

Application
♥ How will you apply this life lesson in your life?

_____

_____

_____

"You cannot serve both God and money."
— Matthew 6:24 (NIV)

LIFE LESSON

48

CAPTURE THE MEMORIES

My family came to visit in Boston this week. What a joy to have them there! What is one of the main attractions to do in Boston with kids? A duck-boat tour! I'd never been on one before and it was so fun to watch the joy on our kids' faces as we traveled the streets of Boston, with our entertaining guide cracking jokes that completely matched our family's wacky sense of humor.

We drove along, learning about the history of Boston and eventually wove our way down past the city's skate park as we drove into the water and went from being a truck on the street to a boat in the water.

Our four-year-old had been with my parents and said my dad told him he would be able to drive the duck boat. Well, let me just say our four-year-old has a tremendously creative mind, and sometimes he shares really awesome stories… that are sometimes believable but definitely *not* true. I told him I didn't think that was part of the plan.

But, as it turns out, he was right! As we drove further out into the water, the driver invited all the kids on the boat to sit and steer it! Stephen and I were able to watch each of our kids take a turn behind the wheel of the duck boat. It was a moment I will always treasure.

In the midst of my treatment, I was able to create and capture fond, lasting memories with my family. I didn't have to let the worries of tomorrow take me away from experiencing the joy that was available for me to share in that day, in that moment. I share this with you because, yes, we all have struggles. Yet we don't have to allow our struggles to stop us from experiencing the moments of joy that are available for us to experience today with our loved ones.

I invite you to join me to…

Pause. Breathe. Pray.

And if we are able, in mind and body, to show up beside our loved ones today, let's do it. May we create and capture memories that will last a lifetime.

And if you're stuck, I get it. I've had depression in life and know the other side of this – where the desire is there but it's impossible to "show up," not only for others, but even ourselves. If that's the case for you, please be sure you reach out to get help. It is humbling, but it will be worth it. *You* are worth it.

LIFE LESSON
48
CAPTURE THE MEMORIES

REFLECTION ~ APPLICATION

Take a moment to…
Pause. Breathe. Pray.

Reflection
♥ Notes to self about this life lesson:

_____

_____

_____

Application
♥ How will you apply this life lesson in your life?

_____

_____

_____

"Let us not love with words and speech but with actions and in truth."
— 1 John 3:18 (NIV)

LIFE LESSON

49

BE SURE TO ENJOY THE VIEW
(EVEN ON YOUR WAY UPHILL)

Every day I pass by charming historic streets in Boston. What I love about this one is the beautiful view from the bottom of the hill. It got me thinking:

This weekend, things shifted and my pain has increased immensely. I don't share this for pity but to be real with you regarding where I am on my walk with cancer. Radiation is taking its toll in my mouth. I have mouth sores in many places now, including on my tongue. Since the majority of my sores are where my obturator sits, it makes some things a little more challenging, like eating – with every swallow my obturator rubs against a sore.

Fatigue has set in from the chemo and radiation, as well. I'm admittedly challenged daily on how to respond to this hill I am climbing. I have had many people say how it's okay for me to feel bad and to say what I'm going through sucks. And I will be the first to say it does suck; but...

Like any hill, if I attempt to climb it focused on the pain it is causing, or *may* cause me, my walk uphill will be that much more challenging. Half the battle (or more!) is what is happening in our minds. If instead I choose to look at the beauty along my walk up the hill, I'll have more peace within. Like the hill in this picture, if I were walking up it, I could think about the physical pain it may cause – or is causing – to climb it; or I can choose to focus my attention on the beautiful brick buildings, the blossoming trees and the bright blue sky.

The same is true with my walk with cancer. I could choose to complain all day and get stuck in the pain, or I can choose to look around and absorb the beauty and blessing along the way.

Yes, I experience pain, and it is real and it is challenging; but I choose to look for the beauty and blessings around me to experience more joy in this process.

It is tempting on days to see the hill, the struggle, the pain, and put my head down as I trudge up that hill. But there are so many people I wouldn't have met, joyful moments I would have missed out on, and blessings given (or received), if I chose to focus on the pain alone. Looking around at the beauty, and seeking God's blessings along the way, is part of my healing, because although my body is in pain and tired, it keeps my Spirit well.

I share this with you because we all have a hill we are climbing. Maybe it has to do with your health, a relationship, finances, career, etc. Whatever your hill, I encourage you to join me to…

Pause. Breathe Pray.

Let's choose to not get caught up in the pain or fast forward to the possibility of what more pain may be like. Let us instead choose to view the hill as a chance to grow stronger, from the inside out. Let us seek the beauty and God's blessings around us – they are there. When we are able to do this, we can have more peace and joy within – even with pain present. Trust me. The hill and the pain, therefore, aren't something to grow angry or frustrated with, but instead something to give thanks for, because they are teachers, helping us grow deeper into the person we were made to be – and they make even the bottom of the hill a beautiful view.

LIFE LESSON
49

BE SURE TO ENJOY THE VIEW
(EVEN ON YOUR WAY UPHILL)

REFLECTION ~ APPLICATION

Take a moment to...
Pause. Breathe. Pray.

Reflection
♥ Notes to self about this life lesson:

_____

_____

_____

Application
♥ How will you apply this life lesson in your life?

_____

_____

_____

"May the God of hope fill you with joy and peace
as you trust in him, so that you may overflow with hope."
– Romans 15:13 (NIV)

185

LIFE LESSON

50

GOD WILL ALWAYS PROVIDE

My faith is an important facet in my life; and part of my daily routine is reading the Bible. Now, if that makes you want to close this book, I understand. A few years ago I would've felt the same way. I've since gained a new view of the Bible and look at it as a collection of historical letters, combined into one book. That perspective was helpful for me to start reading it.

Anyway, in one of the letters, I remember reading about how God will provide. When I had to come up to Boston, I had no idea how we were going to afford anything. We had put ourselves in a good place financially years ago on our debt-free journey; but between medical bills, the stay in Boston and just life, I was unsure how we were going to make it work. But in my prayer time one day, I had a moment of calm and said, "God I will go and trust that you will provide for our needs."

I can't explain it more than that, but as I look at my time here in Boston, every detail was provided for. People made meals for our family; others gifted us a cleaning person; a local company, Healing Meals, made bone broth for me weekly and another local company, Landscape Solutions and Maintenance, donated lawn services to us. My parents surprised us and had our stays in Boston practically covered by family and friends donating their travel points toward it. We were gifted gas gift cards for our travel, and grocery gifts cards that covered my groceries while I was gone during the week. We even had relatives pay for our parking while we were there.

Every act of love from someone confirmed what God promises: He will provide for our needs and He uses people around us to do so.

When I heard of these generous offerings, I often cried grateful tears, overwhelmed by the generous hearts of those around us, and with gratitude that our needs were provided for. I have been able to focus on healing, and we didn't have the weight of those burdens on our shoulders.

I share this because I wholeheartedly believe God has provided for all our needs; we just may be not allocating what has been given to us toward where it needs to be (versus where we want it to go).

What do I mean by that?

For example, how do we rationalize having lottery jackpots worth hundreds of millions of dollars and yet children still go hungry in our world?

I invite you to join me to…

Pause. Breathe. Pray.

And may we each trust our needs will be provided for. Not our desires, but our needs. I'm sure some of you are wondering how those bills stacking up will be paid. I know this idea is easier to listen to than believe. Yet I wholeheartedly believe if we as a society chose to live within our needs, there would be funds available to help others around us who have unmet needs.

Is that our responsibility to take care of each other?

The world tells me no. God tells me yes.

The love that has been poured our way has filled my heart, and I plan to do what is mine to do, to take this love that has been poured into our lives, and scatter it toward others and be a vessel of God's love to help provide for others' needs.

LIFE LESSON
50
GOD WILL ALWAYS PROVIDE

REFLECTION - APPLICATION

Take a moment to…
Pause. Breathe. Pray.

Reflection
  ♥ Notes to self about this life lesson:

_____

_____

_____

Application
  ♥ How will you apply this life lesson in your life?

_____

_____

_____

"God will supply every need of yours according to his riches."
— Philippians 4:19 (ESV)

LIFE LESSON

51

DO WHAT YOU CAN TO SHOW UP FOR OTHERS

One of the toughest parts about being away from my family is I knew going into this I'd be gone on my son's 10th birthday. It broke my heart. He was such a trooper, understanding I would have been there for him if I could, but my schedule that week did not make it possible.

You see, his birthday was on a Tuesday, and that was my chemo day. And every day, Monday through Friday, I had radiation. Typically they administered children's radiation treatments first thing in the morning and appointments later on for adults. The day before his birthday I looked at the schedule and thought, *I have to make it home*. I had to at least ask if I could switch appointments, to at least know I'd done what was mine to do to be there beside my son for his 10th birthday – even if for only a sliver of it.

When I reached out to my radiology team, they said they would see what they could do. And by the grace of God, they were able to switch my appointments so I would get all my treatments in the morning, then hop in the car and get home in time to meet my family for dinner.

On the drive home, I was as giddy as could be. My son had no clue I was on my way and I couldn't wait to see his face and wrap my arms around my now-10-year-old.

When I entered our family's favorite pizza place, he happened to be looking down. I snuck up behind him and said in his ear, "Happy Birthday, Buddy."

My son turned around with a look of shock on his face. He wrapped his arms around me and gave me the biggest hug. He let go for a second, looked at me again, face to face, and then went in for a second hug.

That moment is one I will forever have captured in my heart. Being able to show up for my son on his 10th birthday was a gift for me, but more importantly, for him. I want him, and my other two kids, to know I will do whatever I can to show up for them in life.

I invite you to join me to…

Pause. Breathe. Pray.

And let's ask ourselves if there is something in our schedules we could switch around to be sure to show up for our loved ones. In years, we most likely won't remember the meeting or things scheduled, but will remember our loved ones' faces when we show up for them.

I know I will.

When I was reminiscing with my son about this moment as I revised this chapter, I asked him what life lesson he learned from that experience and he said, "IF YOU DON'T EXPECT SOMETHING, THE REWARD IS GREATER."

I thought that was an extra lesson worth including for you.

LIFE LESSON
51
DO WHAT YOU CAN TO SHOW UP FOR OTHERS

REFLECTION ~ APPLICATION

Take a moment to...
Pause. Breathe. Pray.

Reflection
♥ Notes to self about this life lesson:

Application
♥ How will you apply this life lesson in your life?

"Above all, love each other deeply."
— 1 Peter 4:8 (NIV)

DIVINE APPOINTMENT

9

My children got out of school for the summer on June 20. My last treatment was on June 22, so my parents brought them to Boston to join Stephen and me for the last couple of days. It was a blessing to have them there beside me to close out this chapter in our family's book.

The day before my last treatment, the tall ships were visiting Boston, so we took the kids over to go on them. While we were on one, I passed a man who had an anchor on the pocket of his shirt with the word "HOPE" written within it.

Anchors to me represented hope. Hebrews 6:19, "Hope anchors the soul," was one of my meditations through my mother's treatment and my own walk with cancer. So when I see anchors, they capture my heart. During my treatments, I was blessed to be staying by the water, where old ship anchors lined the streets of Boston... which always made my heart smile.

I asked this man if I could take a picture of his shirt. He said it was fine. I did and we moved along. I actually think my family moved along before me, because they couldn't believe I'd just stopped a total stranger and asked to take a picture of his shirt.

Anyway, when we were about to leave the boat, I saw the man again and noticed he was with a priest. I stopped them and expressed how I am sure that was strange but now seeing who they were, the man with the anchor on his shirt was a brother in the church, I shared why anchors were significant to me.

Two young men of faith in their late 20s stood there listening, and asked if they could give me a blessing as I wrapped up my treatment. Again, I think my family felt a little awkward with this happening on a pier in Boston; but for me, God placed these two men of faith beside me on the day before my treatment ended to bless our family. There they stood beside my family and me and prayed a blessing over us. I am forever grateful for the gift of this divine appointment.

KEEP YOUR EYES AND EARS OPEN
FOR **YOUR** NEXT DIVINE APPOINTMENT

DIVINE APPOINTMENT

10

Before leaving Boston, I wrote thank yous and handed out my kids' book, *A Place for Sam*, to people who blessed me along the way. I found it funny that God had placed a story on my heart the year before I was diagnosed with cancer that was about a puzzle piece, Sam, and how Sam's piece of the puzzle matters. It was a gift because I was able to go around to every person who helped me and thank them and acknowledge how their piece of the puzzle mattered in my walk with cancer.

I had one lovely woman who had checked me into chemo a number of times read my thank-you card while I was in my chemo chair the last day. She started crying and shared with me that she had been thinking recently how she's been doing her job for so long, and wondered if it mattered at all whether she was there in this position. Now she knew her piece of the puzzle mattered.

To be able to affirm that what she does (taking each patient's vital signs prior to their treatment) matters is a gift that will remain in my heart. I was honored to have been able to share the thank yous and books with the administrative assistants, doctors, nurses, volunteers, hotel staff, acupuncturists, massage therapists and other caregivers.

After being home for a number of weeks, to my surprise I received an email from one of the people to whom I had gifted the book. He told me he and his wife had been fostering a child they would soon be adopting. He shared that the book's message really resonated with the child and he would read it several times a week at bedtime to his foster child because its message, about finding his place in the world, resonated with his boy. In November they adopted their son, and he shared with me that they gifted *A Place for*

Sam to the judge, the social worker and a few others who every day are helping foster children, solo puzzle pieces, find connections with their forever homes. He also shared that his son often tells him and his wife how he loves them and will never leave them because he wouldn't fit in any other home. "You are my puzzle piece," he tells them.

Hearing this hit me to the core. To know there is a child out there who has found his forever home, who is encouraged in his heart that he has found his place in the world because of a book I gifted them… that is worth all that I went through for that child to have that peace of heart and mind.

These divine appointments with all these wonderful people were blessings to me on my walk with cancer in Boston. And to know my books were also a blessing to them at such a critical point in their lives is something only God could have orchestrated. It showed me clearly that my walk with cancer had its purpose: to allow these people to use their gifts and skills to bless me, and for me to use my gifts and skills to bless them. And this, my friends, is what life is all about: sharing our gifts with one another to encourage one another and build each other up into the best versions of ourselves.

I will be forever grateful for each person I encountered along my walk with cancer and for the love they poured into my heart, helping me heal, from the inside out.

KEEP YOUR EYES AND EARS OPEN
FOR **YOUR** NEXT DIVINE APPOINTMENT

LIFE LESSON

52

FAITH IS BELIEVING IN SOMETHING YOU CANNOT SEE

One day I was lying on the radiation table, radiation mask on, strapped to the table. I lay there, still, while the radiation team made sure I was in perfect position and all was set for them to start the treatment. As they usually do when they were ready, they ensure I'm all set, then say they'll be right back and exit the room.

I lay there alone in the room on the radiation table, perfectly positioned for the proton beams to do their thing and, hopefully, get those cancer cells they were unable to take out in surgery. The knocking and clicking started, which is a cue the treatment was going to start… but then there is nothing. There is no noise, no light, no scent, nothing I can touch that tells me that the machine is on or working.

When the radiation team came back in, I asked them, "How do I know this is working? There is no noise, light, scent or anything I can touch as proof that it is working."

One team member smiled at me and said, "I understand; but trust me, it is working."

This moment gave me pause.

Trust in something I cannot see, hear, smell or touch. Trust it is working to do what needs to be done, even though there is no physical evidence of it working.

This is faith.

Have faith, Shawn. Have faith not only in God, but in this team and those who created this machine. Have faith that all is working as it needs to, even though you don't see anything at work. Have faith all will be well.

I share this with you because I thought maybe one of you would benefit from hearing the message I relearned that day, that faith is believing in something that you cannot see, hear, touch or smell, but trust in anyway.

I invite you to join me to...

Pause. Breathe. Pray.

And if you have not before, may you consider having faith in God. May we trust that God is working every day in our lives – although we may not see, hear, smell or touch the working of His hands. We may not have the physical proof, but may we have faith anyway.

LIFE LESSON
52
FAITH IS BELIEVING IN SOMETHING YOU CANNOT SEE

REFLECTION ~ APPLICATION

Take a moment to…
Pause. Breathe. Pray.

<u>Reflection</u>
♥ Notes to self about this life lesson:

_____

_____

_____

<u>Application</u>
♥ How will you apply this life lesson in your life?

_____

_____

_____

*"Now faith is confidence in what we hope for
and assurance about what we do not see."*
— Hebrews 11:1 (NIV)

LIFE LESSON

53

THE END IS A NEW BEGINNING

It was surreal as I removed my radiation mask for the last time. I had spent the past seven weeks with it on this table, every day, Monday through Friday. I had spent hours in silence praying for my radiation team, their families and others I met along the way. They never knew it but I had such a sadness saying goodbye to these people, whose days are spent helping cancer fighters, like me.

I was grateful when they said they would walk me out to the waiting room. As the doors opened, I am not sure whether my feet touched the ground as I saw my husband's, children's and parents' smiling faces greeting me with their arms open wide.

We did it! Treatments are over! Woo-hoo!

I hugged each of them with happy tears dancing down my face. Then, together, with the entire radiation team in tow, we all walked over to the bell.

The bell.

For those of you who don't know, at the end of radiation you get to recite a poem and ring a bell three times to conclude your treatments. I had waited seven weeks for this moment. I'd watched many others ring it, including children. My happy tears flowed then as well for those who were done, hopeful they'd never have to do this again. Now, today was my day to ring the bell. To be done. To close this chapter. To move on.

I stood there with a lump in my throat with my family beside me. As I read the words on the plaque:

Ring this bell three times well

Its toll will clearly say

My treatments are done

… emotions of gratitude mixed with relief, came over me. I could barely get out the last two lines…

This course has run

And now I am on my way.

And as my children's hands held the string with mine, together we rang the bell.

Once.

Twice.

Three times.

My treatments were done!

No more chemo!

No more radiation! We can go back home! Together. For good! Woo hoo!

We said goodbye to my radiation team and headed on our way. With the door closing behind us, together we began our new walk, our walk after cancer.

The end of one thing is always the beginning of something new. If you, too, are closing the door on one chapter in your life, I invite you to join me to…

Pause. Breathe. Pray.

May we take the life lessons we learned during our previous walk and use it as wisdom for our new journey ahead.

LIFE LESSON

53

THE END IS A NEW BEGINNING

REFLECTION ~ APPLICATION

Take a moment to...
Pause. Breathe. Pray.

Reflection
♥ Notes to self about this life lesson:

_____

_____

_____

Application
♥ How will you apply this life lesson in your life?

_____

_____

_____

"Because of God's great love we are not consumed,
for his compassions never fail. They are new every morning."
– Lamentations 3:22-23 (NIV)

LIFE LESSON

54

LET GO AND TRUST GOD

Last year, the day before I was diagnosed, I was flying home from Nashville with Stephen after an incredible getaway he'd gifted me for my birthday.

I wrote this blog post on our flight home, but chose not to post it for some reason. Little did I know then how much the message I was writing about was something I needed to be rooted in my heart for the whole year through…

My husband surprised me for my birthday with a trip away for a weekend. We have always wanted to go to Nashville and finally got to! Stephen knows I get travel anxiety and is hopeful my fear of travel will pass in time… and what better way to get over it than to take me away?!

This was our weekend away. The moment our kids drove away with my in-laws, I ugly cried. From there, my stomach got tied in knots, knowing I had to tackle two flights away from my bubble of comfort to enter other people's bubble in Nashville.

With my heart in my throat, I boarded the planes, said my prayers and listened to my favorite music, trying to get my mind away from the dis-ease I was experiencing within.

Once we got there I settled into our new space and had a great weekend with Stephen, exploring Music City.

I sit and write to you often about my journey to live from the inside out, yet I often write to you from my bubble of comfort, where I have lived for 34 of my 38 years of life. Yet today I am writing to you on my travels home from Nashville while 41,000 feet in the air. This is far from my bubble.

As I soar above the clouds right now, I see clearly that I have no control over the outcome and my fear of the unknown is bigger than my faith. I know I have to truly put my life in the hands of others. I have to have faith in the skills of the engineers who designed the planes, the mechanics who built them and care for them, the air-traffic controllers who direct them, pilots who fly them, the flight attendants who are present for our needs on them, and in God's plan.

Sometimes, like right now, I have no choice but to let go and trust God. Yet is sounds much prettier than what it looks like for me, because right now it is a wrestling match in my mind. My stomach is in knots once again, and my heart is beating wildly in my throat. No one around me can see the discomfort I am experiencing within.

Yet I know that sometimes I have to do things I don't want to do to unfold into the person I need to be and to grow deeper in my relationship with God, and others.

Today I have been...

Pausing. Breathing. Praying.

A lot.

Having faith doesn't mean I will always be at peace – although I wish it did. What it does mean is that I believe every experience is an opportunity to grow in faith, trusting that, no matter the outcome, all will be well – in time.

It isn't always pretty, but to have made those memories with Stephen this weekend – and our children with their grandparents – I know is worth it!

This blog post is as significant today as it was last year.

As I move forward, I don't know the outcome – just I like I didn't on my flight. And although I do not know what the future holds, I know who holds the future: God.

My practice is to wake up each day and practice letting go and trusting God – with my heart, my health, my family and my future. It is easier said than done, but I know trusting God is what will bring me the peace I am seeking.

I share this with you today in case you also are unsure of an outcome and are feeling uneasy about it. I offer for you to join me and...

Pause. Breathe. Pray.

May we practice letting go of needing to know and being in control. May we instead surrender ourselves into the loving hands of God who will carry us through, this day, and every day... no matter our circumstances, no matter the outcome. May we let go and trust that God will give purpose to our struggles.

LIFE LESSON

54

LET GO AND TRUST GOD

REFLECTION - APPLICATION

Take a moment to…
Pause. Breathe. Pray.

Reflection
♥ Notes to self about this life lesson:

_____

_____

_____

Application
♥ How will you apply this life lesson in your life?

_____

_____

_____

"Be strong and courageous. Do not be afraid; do not be discouraged,
for God will be with you wherever you go."
– Joshua 1:9 (NIV)

LIFE LESSON

55

LOVE GOD AND LOVE OTHERS

My walk with cancer has taught me so much about what matters in life. The gift cancer gave me is that it cleared away the clutter and gave me eyes to see what matters most in life – which is to love God and love others, starting with those closest to me, my family and friends, and spreading it to the people I pass along the way throughout my day.

My faith in God gave me a solid foundation to stand on during my walk with cancer. The truths in these lessons are all truths I have learned from my relationship with God. These truths are not my own.

My walk with cancer showed me that nothing, no thing, is more important than my family. I have been blessed with a husband who has held true to his vows, loving me in sickness and in health. He showed up for me and our children in ways that are of superhero status. Our three children – who had their own walk with cancer because of me – showed me what courage, faith, strength, resilience and love look and sound like every day, whether I was near or far. Our family, and friends who have become family, walked beside us every step along the way. Every one of these relationships makes my life as rich as it is… rich in love.

God didn't stop my cancer from happening, and therefore I believe my walk with cancer has a purpose. And I wholeheartedly believe, whatever your struggle is, God has a purpose in it for you, too. May we be willing to see beyond our struggle and look at the heart of it, so we can learn what God needs us to gain from the experience.

Now it's time that I walk away from cancer and into another new unknown: life after cancer. I pray these life lessons I've learned will help me on this side of treatment, as well. Whatever comes, I trust with all my heart, soul, mind and strength God will be with me, teaching me more life lessons and gifting me with more divine appointments along my path, to encourage me along the way.

I know this walk after cancer will have its twists and turns, but I believe if I put my faith first, all will be well – for me, and for my family. For me, loving God and loving others comes above everything. For when they do, it gives me perspective and purpose in life.

Wherever you are on your walk, I invite you to take a moment to…

Pause. Breathe. Pray.

And absorb that all these life lessons aren't just for me. They are for you too.

With love and hope,
Shawn

LIFE LESSON
55

LOVE GOD AND LOVE OTHERS

REFLECTION ~ APPLICATION

Take a moment to…
Pause. Breathe. Pray.

<u>Reflection</u>
♥ Notes to self about this life lesson:

_____

_____

_____

<u>Application</u>
♥ How will you apply this life lesson in your life?

_____

_____

_____

"Of all the commandments, which is the most important?'
"The most important one," answered Jesus, "is this…
Love God with all your heart, soul, mind and strength.
The second is this: 'Love your neighbor as yourself.'
There is no commandment greater than these."
— Mark 12:28-31(NIV)

LIFE LESSONS
1 - 55
AND DIVINE APPOINTMENTS

REFLECTION ~ APPLICATION

Take a moment to…
Pause. Breathe. Pray.

<u>Reflection</u>
♥ Notes to self about what I will take away from this book:

_____

_____

_____

<u>Application</u>
♥ How will I take what I have learned and apply it in my
life to help me through my struggle(s)?

_____

_____

_____

"May the Lord bless you and take care of you,
May the Lord smile on you and be gracious to you,
May the Lord show you His favor and give you His peace."
-Numbers 6:24-26 (NLT)

REFERENCES

1. Cooney, Barbara, 1985, Miss Rumphius, Puffin Books
2. Flint, Annie Johnson, (1866-1932), God Hath Not Promised poem
3. Lucado, Max, 2013, God Came Near, Nashville, TN, Thomas Nelson

ACKNOWLEDGEMENTS

A heart full of thank to...

Stephen, Kate, Gavin and Matthew, for your patience as I transition back to life on this side of cancer and for giving me grace and space to write this book this year as part of my healing. I love you all more than words!

My Dad, for capturing this heartfelt, authentic moment on the cover between Stephen and I in Acadia a couple months after my treatment ended. To view other beautiful moments my dad has captured visit www.secretlakephotography.com.

My Mom and Rita M. Reali, both cancer survivors, who edited this book for me. My Mom is not for hire but if you'd like to connect with Rita, visit: www.persnicketyproofreader.wordpress.com.

Mary Leahy, my APRN, for being present with me and sending me to an ENT after our first visit. Also, to her staff for their perseverance with my case.

Dr. Tessema, my ENT,and his staff and team, for taking care of me like a member of their own family.

Dr. Emerick, my surgeon, Dr, Chan, my radiation oncologist, Dr. Clark, my oncologist and their staff and teams at Mass Eye and Ear and Mass General, for your presence, help in healing and continued care.

Dr. Jackson, for using your skills to help people like me have the ability to speak and eat every day with greater ease.

My radiation team, for greeting me with kindness and compassion daily.

To the staff where I stayed for the seven weeks, thank you for your friendship and hospitality.

To every person that cared for Stephen, our children and me in any way shape or form, thank you for being a light in the midst of the darkness.

CONNECT WITH SHAWN

Shawn wrote this book as part of her healing the year after her treatments ended. Her hope is that the life lessons she learned through her walk with cancer would help others through their walk with cancer, or other life struggles. She would love to connect with you to hear what line from *Our Struggles Have Purpose* has encouraged, inspired and/or infused hope into your heart, and how it has helped you along your walk.

To share with Shawn you can email her at:
 - shawnelizabethgeorge@gmail.com

Or connect with her on social media at:
  𝐟 @shawnelizabethgeorge

  ⃝ @shawnelizabethgeorge

  🐦 @shawnelizabethg

And if you choose to share insights from the book on social media, use #OSHP so Shawn can read those too!

To continue to receive Shawn's inspirational messages connect with her at:

WWW.SHAWNELIZABETHGEORGE.COM